The Gold Edition

2010 Poetry Collection

The Gold Edition represents our student authors as accurately as possible.
Every effort has been made to print each poem
as it was submitted with minimal editing
of spelling, grammar, and punctuation.
All submissions have been formatted to this compilation.

Published by
The America Library of Poetry
P.O. Box 978
Houlton, ME 04730
Website: www.libraryofpoetry.com
Email: generalinquiries@libraryofpoetry.com

Printed in the United States of America.

THE AMERICA
LIBRARY OF POETRY

ISBN-10   0-9773662-5-1
ISBN-13   978-0-9773662-5-5

Contents

Poetry by Division

The Gold Edition

... In memory of Vogglyne Thomas
December 3, 1998 – July 28, 2010
(Student Author)

My Home
by Vogglyne Thomas

My home
Is so nice
It has lots of space to play
Sometimes it's quiet
I like spending time in here
It's my home
And I love it

Foreword

There are two kinds of writers in the world.
There are those who write from experience,
and those who write from imagination.
The experienced, offer words that are a reflection of their lives.
The triumphs they have enjoyed, the heartaches they have endured;
all the things that have made them who they are,
they graciously share with us, as a way of sharing themselves,
and in doing so, give us, as readers, someone to whom we may relate,
as well as fresh new perspectives
on what may be our common circumstances in life.
From the imaginative,
come all the wonderful things we have yet to experience;
from sights unseen, to sounds unheard.
They encourage us to explore the limitless possibilities
of our dreams and fantasies,
and aid us in escaping, if only temporarily,
the confines of reality and the rules of society.
To each, we owe a debt of gratitude;
and rightfully so, as each provides a service of equal importance.
Yet, without the other, neither can be truly beneficial.
For instance, one may succeed in accumulating a lifetime of experience,
only to consider it all to have been predictable and unfulfilling,
if denied the chance to chase a dream or two along the way.
Just as those whose imaginations run away with them never to return,
may find that without solid footing in the real world,
life in fantasyland is empty.
As you now embark, dear reader,
upon your journey through these words to remember,
you are about to be treated to both heartfelt tales of experience,
and captivating adventures of imagination.
It is our pleasure to present them for your enjoyment.
To our many authors,
who so proudly represent the two kinds of writers in the world,
we dedicate this book, and offer our sincere thanks;
for now, possibly more than ever,
the world needs you both.

Paul Wilson Charles
Editor

Editor's Choice Award

The Editor's Choice Award is presented
to an author who demonstrates not only
the solid fundamentals of creative writing,
but also the ability to illicit an emotional response
or provide a thought provoking body of work
in a manner which is both clear and concise.

You will find "Teenage Eyes"
by Caeli Faisst
on page 217 of *The Gold Edition*

2010
Spirit of Education

For Outstanding Participation

Our Lady
of
Calvary School

Philadelphia, Pennsylvania

Presented to participating students and faculty
in recognition of your commitment
to literary excellence.

Division I

Grades 3-5

Balloon
by Patrick Saythavy

The balloon is green
In the bright sky at sundown
Floating through the sky.
Floating down the sky
Children catching the balloons
Pop! goes the balloon.
Children crying loud
Their mothers get more balloons
Children stop crying.

Night Time
by Jerry Zhang

During the night,
There is no light.
You would be scared,
But also be aware.
And it is a great sight

Two Friends
by Katelyn Parr

There was a little girl named Katelyn.
She had a friend named Payton.
Katelyn bought a puppy.
Payton bought a guppy.
Katelyn wanted a snow cone.
Then Katelyn and Payton went home.

My Ski Trip
by Brooklyn Bartezak

I went skiing, I had a great time
One day I went to ski school and it was fun
I said good–bye to my teacher
We went back to the condo, ate and went to bed
I got up on Wednesday and went shopping with my dad and sisters
We left Colorado on Saturday and got back home on Sunday

Fire Everywhere
by Angel Moore

I am in a world of peace,
But there's fire everywhere
I am under water,
Still fire everywhere
"Where is the fire coming from?"
I scream to myself when I'm in bed
I do not see the world of peace,
For there is fire everywhere

Being Yourself
by Michael Hafferty

Being yourself is the key
To finding your own individuality.
It doesn't matter what you wear
You don't even have to care.
You're always better off being your own
Instead of being someone's clone.

The Sun
by Alicia Henley

I love the sunshine
The sun is so nice to me
I love the sunshine.
The sun is a star
I love it in the summer
It is very nice.
The sun is so nice
But it gives me a sunburn
Sometimes not so nice.

Hunting and Fishing
by Will Matthews

I like to hunt, and fish, and play basketball!
When I play basketball, I think of fishing!
And when I'm hunting, I think of basketball!

Monkey, Monkey
by Ethan Berg

Monkey, Monkey on the wall
Monkey, Monkey is so tall
Monkey goes into the hall!
Penguin, Penguin in the hall
Penguin, Penguin sees Monkey, Monkey–
Penguin says, "Hi."
Now Monkey, Monkey said, "Time to go back to the wall."

Equal
by Valerie Chu

White or colored,
One true rule to remember,
All are equal

Miguel
by Monica Rodriguez

I like my brother, Miguel
At one year old, he is so cute
I love his chubby cheeks
And his lips are as soft as the finest cotton
But his teeth are as sharp as the razor–edged rocks of Earth!
They dig into your skin and make you scream!
When he sees the door open, he pouts and wails
Until you take him outside and then he will not come in!
On the bright side though,
He loves me more than anybody and I love him too!

Rose
by Melina De La Loza

A pink rose that glows at night
But is as dark as night when light!
A purple rose as dark as night
But as bright as day when light!
A red rose shines in Heaven this night–
And it feels so right to be in Heaven tonight!

The Eagle
by Paige Smith

The eagle soars through the sky.
Seeking food here and there.
When its food is spotted
From the sky with its sharp eye.
There is no stopping it.
Its food cannot escape
From its deadly sharp claws.
Of which it's carried.
Through the cold night.
It seeks.
Its food.

Wonderland
by Joshua Elwood

A giant blowing blanket burying the terrain
This snow stitched on Maine
Coming and going, unlike friendship
Some people having a snow covered stick
Everyone wonders about this wonderland
Filled with snow, not sand
Blankets and blankets of snow
And all people know

Evening Song
by Kirsten Bernhardt

The burning sun sinks silently behind clouds
Shades of lilac, puce, crimson, vermilion, and gold paint the radiant skies
A "V" of geese flies by, hoping to catch the upward crowds
The sea lets out a heavy sigh
Palm trees whisper on the breeze
The day is finally concluding
Residue of a sand castle, does a wave seize
The storm clouds farther east are brooding
Darker and darker it becomes
An alabaster moon now delivers a hazy glow
Its heart sounds like the somber beating of a distant drum
What is its story, why does it woe
Let us look at the resting world once more
The next day will open up a new door

Home Time
by Kyle Earle

Cozy and warm
It smells like cinnamon
Just the way I would like it to be
My home

Trash
by Carter Carlson

Oh, please don't tell my mother,
Or my little brother,
For I had a weird task,
Why did I bother to ask?
It gave my nose a rash,
For the task is I had to take out our stinky trash!
As soon as I smelt this junk,
I vomited on my brother's bunk,
Don't worry, I cleaned off the gunk.

Untitled
by Anna Riesenberg

Clouds are up there
Sitting in the sky
Floating through the air
Almost like they can fly
They come in all sizes and shapes
Some are flat and thin
Others are small and round like grapes,
Or pointy like a pin
Clouds can be dark and gray
They can also be fluffy and white
Clouds can appear in the day
And disappear at night
When they go away it's a shame
But they are not to blame

Cancer
by Shyann Green

Cancer, cancer it hurts us all
Breast cancer, lung cancer
Makes you feel like an old rag doll,
But my, oh my, how some survive!
Colon cancer, liver cancer, it hurts us.
But we survive when times are tough.
Like now when my family is sick
It's really rough.
- I dedicate this poem to my grandma, who has breast cancer.

Useless Things
by Will Perez

Glasses without a lens
A chicken coop without hens
A pen without ink
A boat that doesn't sink
A pencil without lead
A room without a bed
A person without a shoe
A man that just got sued
A truck without a wheel
An orange without a peel
A math book without pages
A zoo without cages
A house without a light
A man that lost his might
A lid without a cap
A tree without any sap
A closet without a broom
A house that went ka-boom

Going Fishing
by Paula Nordstrom

When I'm out on the water I feel so free
So I take out my fishing pole, I reel it out
And when I catch a fish, I reel it in
I feel so great and when I hold a fish, it feels like a trophy
And when I go home, I tell everybody
And I can't wait to go fishing again

I Made a Mistake
by Christopher Dekeyser

I was making a pie
I made a mistake and cooked a fly
I was going to my school
I made a mistake, I went to the pool
I was going to play chess
I made a mistake, I made a mess
I was going to the pet store to buy a cat
I made a mistake and bought a bat
I wanted a toy
I made a mistake and got a boy

Tiny
by Hunter Stevens

Puppy
Small, brown
Looking, sitting, jumping
Barking loudly at me
Barking eating, playing
Cute, fun
Tiny

Riding Free
by Paloma Pacho

The wind blows on my face,
While I am riding free.
Running, prancing, galloping,
That's how we go,
But we are not going fast or slow.
There are miles to go,
And places to see that I don't know.
When will we get there?
What will we see?
Someday I'll be free.
But, don't get upset with me,
Soon you'll see, someday I'll be free.

Wolfie
by Zoe Zimmerman

Wolfie
Smelly, busy
Purring, hissing, biting
Sleeping all the time
Laying, cheerful
Cat

Mischievous Ariel
by Samantha Summers

I lay in bed,
Light shining through my window.
But, it is not what awakens me.
Scratching, scratching,
Waiting for my return,
Waiting for play
Waiting for attention.
My angel, mischievous Ariel

Reading
by Abbigail Miramontes

I was reading on the couch, my book-nook
I read all day, they said, "You're a bookworm."
In my book, kids are trying to catch a mean crook
"It's time to stop!" Mom says, she sounds firm
No stopping! Not now, the page had to turn!
I discovered a pot going bang, mate
Mom was mad, "Time to go, or you won't learn!"
Oops! Today's school, I hope I'm not late!
When we got to school, I raced down the hall
When I got to class, my hair was not neat
My nice teacher asked, "Were you at the mall?"
"No," I replied, looking at my small feet
Reading is like being in a new land
When I'm older, I won't be doing band!

God
by Elannia Lake

God is my rock, protector, and fortress
While I'm with Him, Satan won't ever hurt me
He looks inside, past how you look and dress
God is greater than I ever will be
He is a wall that will never crumble
A hard rock that Satan can't ever break
God picks me up every time I stumble
He is the best, make no mistake
There are some people that are not Christians
I know it sounds sad, but it is still true
We must preach to all of every nation
I might be a preacher. How about you?
God has some plans that you may not expect
If you're lost, then listen, God will direct

Fire
by Elaina Gullick

Fire's a blood thirsty beast
Burning wood's to be its feast,
As it sits atop a throne of ash
That was scorched a might too fast,
For its torched body masked in flame
From its devilish burning game.

Kids
by Nathaniel Ajel

Little rascals that give life some fun
The ones that love to play in the sun
Parents love them no matter how old
Even if they have a very nasty cold
They go crazy no matter where they are
To them their parents are their stars
Handle these gifts with lots of care
Sometimes they don't want to share
No matter where, who, or what they did
To everyone, these gifts are called kids

Baby Blue
by Joselyn Jaime

Baby blue is the smell that you get when a cookie comes straight from the oven
Baby blue feels like the soft fur of a bunny's back
Baby blue is the sound of a classical flute
Baby blue is the taste of sweet sugary candy
Baby blue looks like cotton, sweet and fluffy

My Daddy
by Caden Holochwost

Dad
Friendly, playful
Loving, caring, helping
Daddy cares for me
Daddy

Butterflies
by Cece Cannata

Flying butterflies
Fluttering little creatures
Light and delicate

Nighttime Walk
by Pia Satana

The sounds of the night are so crystal and clear
Filled with the rustle of leaves in the trees
Dark in the night there is nothing to fear
So peaceful, so quiet without humming bees
While walking in darkness
You hear a loud howl
Yet you know that it's harmless
Then you see the owl
He softly gazes into your eyes
Then swish, "Hoot, hoot!"
So graceful he is, look at him rise
Amazed by this splendor, you sit on a root
I wish I were not alone with just me
On this magnificent night, I wish for thee.

Varnack and Lolly
by Ellie Higgins

Varnack is a hot sand dune with sharp hits by the wind,
Lolly is a colorful field of bright and exotic flowers.
Varnack is a blood shot red,
And Lolly is the color of baby blue.
When it comes to objects ...
Varnack is a sharp and rough boulder,
And Lolly is a crisp orange rose.
If Varnack was a person,
He would probably be the old mad person
And Lolly would be the young loving mother calling her children.
Varnack is the wind biting at your nose,
And Lolly is the cool summer breeze.
Varnack is sharp and sour,
Lolly is the fluffy sweet taste.
When it comes to music ...
Varnack is the ear piercing metallic rock,
And Lolly is soothing classical music.
As a feeling ...
Varnack is the sharp, painful feeling,
Lolly is like the touch of a cotton cloud.
Varnack is the annoying teenager,
And Lolly is the sister always trying to help people.
Those are all the differences between Varnack and Lolly.

Sweetness
by Amy Bezek

Sugar, toys, candy, pets
They are not like a T-Rex
Mom, Dad, animals, flowers
All have sweetness and wonderful powers
Ocean, games, happiness, books
Make me get caught on sweetness' hook
Family, hugs, kisses, love
The gentle flight of a dove
Caring, soothing, gentle, soft
Cats sleeping in a barn loft
Perfume, soda, babies, home
Aren't gruff like a garden gnome
What is sweetness? Do you know?
All the above is a show

A Puppy's Love
by Joyce Zamorano

A puppy's love has many things,
Curious, caring to one another.
A puppy's love can have fun friendship,
"Woof, woof!" Playful cheers here and there.
When all the fun's done,
You run, run, run to the small comfy bed.
A sleepy puppy dreams wonderful dreams.
A puppy's love can have many more things!

Tasty Pie
by Faisal Safdari

When I was shy, pie came into my life.
I lied about eating the last piece of pie,
Then I would sigh because I lied.
In the high sky, I would see pie clouds
And dreamed about flying high in the sky.
At the Thai restaurant nearby, I was wearing fancy clothes and a tie
And pie fell on my tie.
Why pie, why?
Your apple, banana, pumpkin, and creamy goodness.
My madness makes me love pie even more.
Raging rabbits, who cares!

Life of a Shoe
by Madeline Scott

Sloppily thrown on, we move,
Gliding, then hitting; gliding, then hitting the misty grass
Gliding and then we soar down to the tangly, green jungle
Once again I spring up, we trade off
We both hit the green and rest
Our lacey hair dangles down to the misty earth
We move, pushing away from the ground
And slamming against it once more; moving faster, faster, faster
I can't control the speed
We start to slow down
We get thrown off sloppily as our tongues hang out.

The Krazy Animal World
by Paola Moreno

A krazy world where the kangaroos roar
And the fish sing and much, much more.
Where the cows swim and the birds flop,
Where the monkeys eat yogurt with a cherry on top.
Where the platypuses fly,
And the polar bears eat pie.
Where the sharks walk on land with fins.
Where koalas live in igloos, and where dolphins
Carry iPods, and in the deep blue sea
You can see a giraffe looking up at me
The rabbits are blue and born with the flu
In a shoe that's laces are sealed with some glue,
With a hat on too.
I told you enough my friend,
So know it's the end.

The Dream
by Zack Bookwalter

I had a dream
A dream of deep love
And this is what happened.
There was a girl with brunette hair, a pink shirt, a skirt,
And a smile on her face
She sang to the stars
She sang like an angel
And all the decision to do it that way
The wind in her hair
And time to clean it
And that's when I met her
The love of my dream
I see her all day
And listen to her songs she sang
With all the world at her side
And sat to side to see the world glisten
With all the people in it
She sat at the side of the world
She had eyes the color of gold
And I love her.

Dawn
by Jenna Himawan

The sun is shining,
Oh, so very bright.
The birds are chirping,
Pretty as dawn's light.
There's pink and there's red,
Which makes a nice sky.
I tilt up my head
To look up so high.
Owls are asleep.
Animals will wake.
You hear the chicks cheep.
Fish leap from a lake.
Now we welcome dawn,
Since the night is gone.

Sub, Sub
by Lane Beanblossom

Sub, sub
Why so mean?
Sub, sub
Why so green?
Mr. Hulk, please
Don't get mad.
I promise our class
Will stop being bad!

Where Is Love?
by Blake Eslick

Why is love so far behind?
I thought it was just next in line!
I lost my love so long ago
I don't even remember the great white snow!
Now it's time, I have to go
I'll see you in the morning snow!

Spring Days
by Noah Mix

Birds build nests for shelter outside on a big oak tree
As the sun shines outside so bright
And flowers begin to bloom in the springtime day
And the smell of fresh dew that reflects a rainbow
That makes you laugh in the morning day
As a blue bird flies by
You hear the pecks of a woodpecker break
As a pine tree slowly dissolves by the minute
You hear the song of a hummingbird
That makes you want to sing
You see a Frisbee fly on by
Then you hear a lullaby for a body
In a springtime rain
Full of love for the child that laughs
At a butterfly so beautiful and calm

Basketball
by Delanie Tipton

Ball, ball, get that ball!
Getting that ball
Is fun for all!
Come on ya'll, get that ball!

A Frozen Lake
by Emma Hall

A frozen lake sits upon a cloud
Sparkling in the sun, glimmering like a diamond
There are hills in the distance
Rising and falling
Like waves in a faraway ocean
All is silent under a ruby red sunset
The trees are going to sleep
A frozen lake sits upon a cloud
In a far, faraway place

What I Found In My Desk
by Julia Greenfield

A bright aqua pen with too much ink,
A rotting egg that really stinks.
Some itchy dog hairs I shaved a week ago,
An old broken Frisbee I meant to throw.
A gooey piece of brown moldy bread,
A Barbie doll with a chewed off head.
An expired ticket to a magic place,
A mask that looked like it fell on its face.
And one more thing that I found–
It made me embarrassed; I looked at the ground.
What I found:
Dear ~~~~,
Clean this mess during recess!
–Teacher

If I Were In Charge of the World
by Sally Kashala

If I were in charge of the world
I would cancel
Unscented candles
Headless Barbie dolls
Words that start with Z
Books that I can't read
Asparagus and old cheese
Some more old things
Children that can't say please
And birds with no wings.
If I were in charge of the world
I would cancel
Drunk teens
Bad tasting tea
Cars with no speed
A friend of Billy Jean's
And pots with no beans.
If I were in charge of the world
I would cancel
Shoes with no lace
A pogo stick race
Erasers that don't erase
And people with a lot of hate.

I Am ...
by Shakira Childers

I am different in many ways
I wonder will the Earth ever stop moving
I hear God speaking to my soul
I see needy people on the streets
I want to see my father
I am different in many ways
I pretend to run away to Detroit
I feel my father rubbing his hand against my face
I touch the Earth and make it stop moving for once
I worry that I will die
I cry for my father
I am different in many ways
I understand that people are dying for food
I say that everyone is the same
I dream that my father is in pain, bad pain
I try to save people that are dying
I hope that my father will come see me someday
I am different in many ways

Macie and Gracie
by Edwin Palma

One day Macie wouldn't let Gracie out,
So she began to pout.
He started to growl,
So she started to bow,
And the next thing,
She wouldn't let him out.

Around the World
by Cassie Scudder

One small baby girl is born in California.
While another tiny baby is sleeping peacefully
Other children's teddy bears are torn.
Two children are running a mile
A small boy is eating corn
And a baby girl is on freezing tile
It does not matter who you are around the world or neighbors
Big like an elephant or small like an ant.

Ocean
by Deoviae Jackson

The ocean waves
Twirling around me
At the bottom
I feel happy and cheerful.

Nature Lovers
by Jessica Ward

Nature lovers love to uncover,
The secret of nature.
Nature lovers are just like others,
They honor their fathers and mothers.
Nature lovers love to be in the sun,
Out playing and having fun.
Nature lovers are full of joy,
When they hear that story, about a baby boy.
Nature lovers, love insects and plants too,
Especially when they are brand new.
Nature lovers are people just like me and you,
We respect the world around us and our families too.

Birds
by Yoonju Pak

How would life be without birds?
Without your morning song all sweet and soft?
Without their soft feathers and beautiful colors?
Without a pet you need not to buy to keep.
How would life be I wonder?
No pretty paintings of the beautiful birds,
No sight for us to try to conquer.
No matter how many times we see it,
We treasure the sight again and again.
No more fascinating pictures of birds in midair,
No more gazing, of the graceful, beautiful birds.
It would hurt me so, to see one bird,
Then never one again.

DeQueen
by Nicolette Leeper

DeQueen is a town I miss
DeQueen is a love of mist
The park is cool
The park is clean
The park is better than anything
On the monkey bars
I climb like monkeys
Through the trees

Me and Spring
by Kristina Judd

As spring comes, winter goes, snow melts
And the fresh grass sprouts
Newly hatched birds learn to fly by their moms
Bees fly friendly, looking around for flowers
To get pollen to make honey
As I lay there thinking how much I love spring!!

Winter
by Chankrisna Khun

Winter is like
That golden breeze
On a hot summer's day
It's not too cold or hot.

Swimming Pool
by Dean Koutsoulis

Swimming,
Swimming,
Swimming,
Swimming,
Swimming,
Swimming pool,
I want to go swimming.
So I wait
And wait, and wait, and wait,
To go swimming!

The Bear
by Anthony Mac

There once was a bear
Who had no hair
And trampled a frog
When he got stuck in a bog,
But didn't even care.

Summer
by Tiana Loyd

Summer is awesome
There's no breeze, but I don't care
I love it so much!

War Through Rivers of Blood
by Anna Lyashenko

War has no cease
With torment and hatred
Pain and rejection
Death and murder
And much more
War ends with rivers of blood
Running across the battlefield
Into a stream yet to cease
They only want to kill the peace
Those who fought and innocent Jews who were burnt by Hitler
The wars in the past and the wars in the future
Don't help with peace building
Many believe the end is near,
But look all around us,
All this pain and rejection
Torment and hatred
Death and murder
And much more
It mocks us does it not?
May as well wallow in war
Never to find peace
If only there was peace in the world
Just what we need in this world is peace,
Wonderful peace

The Shark
by Bridgette Magness

Kenny is a shark
That would love to be bark
He liked to go to bed
Right before he got fed
Kenny was afraid of the dark

Compost
by Eric Mahoney

Compost is yummy,
Just right for my tummy!
It is healthy and wealthy in rotten carrots,
And once was eaten by some parrots.
This stuff has so much power!
(The poet who wrote this is a flower).

Meadow
by Arica McGruther

Meadow
In the springtime
In the midnight sky
The wind, the whisper, the roses
I see shadows, stars, and new moon
Walking, whispering
It waits for me to come
I will feel happy

Rough Days
by Cortlyn Meadows

Sometimes it can be tough,
Sometimes you can just about have enough.
Though you should wake up,
Put some tea in your cup.
Because your day might not be rough.

School
by Jacob McDermott

School
Fun, Awesome
Learning, teaching, playing
School is really fun
Home

The Ocean
by Destiny Ortiz

Here I am, just about to walk in the deep ocean.
Right when I walked in, I felt the cold water rush between my legs,
But it does not bother me.
As I got deeper, I could feel the tiny fish rush between my legs.
Soon I feel something twirling around my legs.
Ouch! A jelly fish stung me!
Now I am running back to shore.
I stopped and turned around to say goodbye to the ocean.

My Limerick
by Sofia Hawes

There was a young boy in Maui
Who got a gigantic owie
He said to his friend,
"I'll just surf a big bend"
And the people just said wowie

One Sock
by Michael Hopper

There once was sock
That lived on a rock.
He got a big knot
From a big man named Lot
The knot got bigger
The sock hit a rock.

The Little Boy Who Had Too Much Stuff Around
by Nicolas Porter

I am a little boy.
I live with my dad.
His name is Nick.
Nick likes to kick and pick.
His home is a field with a lot of boom.
He has a lot of shooting.
Every day there's poo.
Poo always goes to new things.
Those new things involve shooting and tooting.
The tooting always led to the devil's walking stick.
Then the town stops,
And everybody went up to Jupiter
'Cause they were already in space.

My Feelings
by William Remitz

My feelings are happy
But they feel unhappy at the same time
Like when I'm mad, I'm glad, and very sad
And when I'm very bored
And feel like a broken in half cord
And I don't want to play at all today
When it is cold out, it feels warm to me without a doubt
Although when it is warm, I feel cold and also very old
I want to say hello,
But I have to say goodbye

Bullet
by Valina Rogers

I hear the shot, then
Feel the bullet pierce my chest
I cry out in pain, but no one
Was there to help me.

Collection
by Navjyot Sandhu

The bittersweet flavor
Of lost, dear, sweet memories
His lips seem to burn.
They are destroying
Everything within their sights
They are tornadoes.
Boom! goes the cannon
Somebody falls, such is war
Nightmarishly real

If You Say You Know Nothing
by Luke Vu

If you say you know nothing,
That means you know something.
Because you know that you know nothing.
You should think about what you say.

Playing Baseball
by Jacob Torres

As I walk onto the green plains
I feel as nervous as a mouse that just saw a cat.
When I place my bat over home plate,
I see the ball charging at me as if it was a bull.
I swing my bat like a lumberjack would swing his axe.
Whack! The ball goes soaring like an eagle and suddenly it hits the ground.
I slide to first base with ease as if it was a Slip-n-Slide.
In amazement, I realize the ball is on the ground. I run to second base.
As the smell of freshly cut grass lingers across my face,
I hear my team crying out to me to run to third base.
So I charge to third base and don't stop.
The last thing I remember is seeing my hand on home plate
As the catcher touches me with the ball.
I look up to the umpire as he yells, "Safe!"

Spring
by Clover Vanderheiden

The trees are growing.
The sun is setting so fast.
Spring is coming.

Hope
by Neeharika Vogety

A feeling of hope and joy
Surrounds my darkened happenings
Hope makes it something to enjoy
Takes away the sadness in everything
When I feel alone
Like nobody's at home
I count on hope
To make me cope
Life can be blessed,
Life can be sad
But with hope on my side,
I just feel glad

The American Revolution
by Justin Wang

The American Revolution
Made America a nation.
The English king came across the sea
After the Americans dumped the tea.
So many redcoats
Came across in boats.
Paul Revere protected Lexington
He was a patriot like Washington.
"The redcoats are coming," he would shout
Oh! How much the minute men would pout!
After the long war, we built many a city
Quickly in this land of peace and prosperity.

The Seagull
by Nikolas Williamson

The seagull is a handsome bird.
That looks so spick and span.
It's easy to forget that he's a seashore garbage man.
And I wonder if he can fly in the sand?
But I also think he is bland like a band in the sand.

My Pet Elephant
by Bailey Gibbs

For my birthday Mom got me
An elephant
He is very mean
Thank goodness I didn't take
Him out for Halloween

The Path To Freedom
by Tiffany Wu

I ain't gonna say that my skin's not all black,
I say it proud, even if it means a whack.
I've heard tha' some people follow the North Star,
Some have been freed, but others have been black tarred.
I've seen some others try to escape,
After the very next stormy day.
I've gotten a great escape plan,
An' I know just the woman.
That's the famous Harriet Tubman,
She can do anything, yes, she can.
The next time the gal comes,
Wi' be like rays of the sun.
I'll follow the North Star, shining in the sky,
I'll be all freed, followin' my will, or I'll just die.
I have to have a lot of good spirits and hopes,
From this I have energy to climb o'er slopes.
It's been twenty long years after those slave days,
And now I can work anywhere, even cafés.
I am grateful for all those white men who offered to help,
They were nice to us, even if they could only offer kelp.

My Apple Tree
by Jessica Xing

She stood, proudly, along the white fence,
Her bark is probably as old as me,
She grew with me when I was a baby to what I am now
This is the story of my apple tree
A mere sapling she was when I was little,
My dad planted her on the soft black soil
He smiled, and he called her my apple tree
I watched her grow, branch by branch, leaf by leaf,
I played under her, I read under her,
I was always there to care for her,
The tree that I cherished as my dearest friend
Time passed, and my friend grew along with me
She towered over me with her long branches.
Her bark was dark brown and her light pink flowers,
Showered her with a beauty none could put in words
Now, the tree is as old as I am,
She bears yellow apples that I would eat
I savor every one of those apples I ate
Not only because of the flavor,
But because this is my apple tree

My Dreams
by Ciyin Oliveira

My dreams, my dreams they come alive
My dreams, my dreams just close your eyes
Empty your mind, you don't know what you'll find
My dreams, my dreams they come alive
My dreams, my dreams look with your third eye
Focus on being and then you'll start dreaming
My dreams, my dreams look at them go
My dreams, my dreams they take off and flow
Fly with the eagles, take off into the sky
And your dreams will come alive.
Your dreams, your dreams think of one thing
And that one thing may bring a new world

Summary

Summer
by Abagail Fitts

Playing in the sun
Splashing in the pool
Summer is so much fun
And there's no school
Sandals and flip flops
Beaches and bays
Some kids like to swim
Some kids like to walk
But either way
We'll have a good time

When I Ride
by Chloe' James

When I ride my sorrows are washed away,
My fears are gone and everything is okay,
I feel my blood pumping as fast as can be,
I ride over the hill smiling, happy and free.
When I ride the world seems to have no end,
My everlasting joy is beyond the extend,
I pet Imber and tell her goodbye,
Remembering the limit is the sky.

Butterfly
by Gweneth Moore

I dance through hair, eat dust, love flowers.
My dainty steps lead nature to its place.
I always do my dance through wind.
I travel far but my journey never ends.
I feel the best when I am loved.
I love my Earth so when I'm near
I always give a chance to say, "I love you, Earth!"
My words ring out, just like a harp.
And the melody drifts me away.
My life is still singing, even when I'm passed away.

Mr. Blue Man
by Vaibhav Gopal

Mr. Blue Man has glasses.
Mr. Blue Man has face painting.
Mr. Blue man has blue hair.
Blue Man has a blue shirt.
Blue Man has blue pants.
It makes me happy.

America
by Logan Grady

Roses are red,
Violets are blue.
I love America,
So should you.

Apples
by Shraddha Thanukrishnamurthy

Juicy, juicy apples
Round as a ball
Red as a cherry
Smooth as a table
Sweet as sugar
Make it into juice
Make it into sauce
Make it into muffins
Or make it into pies.

The U.S.A.
by Andrew Forman

I'm bored
I have nothing to do
The U.S.A. lost in overtime
I am very frustrated
But at least I can rhyme
The sky is looking blue
I'd like to go outside,
But I can't find my shoe.

Time Slithers Like a Serpent
by Anna Roethig

Time slithers like a serpent
In fantasy lands
It overpasses
The hourglasses
And turns the tide of sands
Time slithers like a serpent
Where people cannot see
It creeps past
The shipyard mast
And through the turquoise sea
Time slithers like a serpent
Through the flower beds
It won't stop
Only hop
And nothing can be said
Time slithers like a serpent
Into the town's end
To the sea
And by the tree
Only tomorrow, it shall send

Winter Wolves
by Erika Wolf

Sound asleep until
The crying of wolves came to
My winter window

Friendship
by Maria Aranda

Friendship
Happy, playful
Singing, laughing, enjoying
Things may not be as they seem
Hating, hurting, feelings
Cruel, mean
Enemies

My Big Bay Horse
by Katarina Wulstein

As I ride my big bay horse,
Her mane is so coarse,
As it whips me in the face
As we are on our long chase,
I whistle to the sound of hoof beats
To make sure my rhythm meets
She glides like a snowflake
Without making a mistake
As I return from my chase,
There is a problem I must face
I must clean up her poo
Underneath her shoe
The day has finally come to an end
It will soon come again
I must go to sleep
Before I leap

NFL
by Zeb Stevens

I want to be a lot of things
But not a scientist or even a mayor
I want to work in the NFL
And be a football player
And if they pick me for the Saints
I will be on quite a roll
And bring them back for a win
In the Super Bowl
And in this experience I will make lots of friends
Go back the next season and do it again
I'm running with the ball
Tackle me–oh darn!
I heard something crack
I think I broke my arm–oh well
Now everyone can see
A NFL player is still what I want to be!

Rain
by Jimmy Zhu

On a day when gray clouds are in the sky
Waves hit the shore
And the city experiences a downpour

The Pigeon
by Ashley Hay

Nobody likes him, that is true
He's big, he's fat, and ugly, too
He'll drink the dew off the car
And stick to you like tar
He flies around on great big wings
And acts like he's the king of kings
Yes, you're absolutely right
The pigeon is this terrible fright
He's a rat with wings and nobody wants him tonight

Feelings
by Sweta Parija

Happiness includes a rainbow,
Faster than the tango.
The sadness includes a waterfall,
The water you can't haul.
Excitement is the scream of joy,
Like when you got a toy.
Angriness shows mad,
Someone has been bad.
Shocking is dazzling,
As if a snake has been rattling.
Fatigue is exhaustion,
When running be cautious.
Joy is a mysterious gift.
It raises your smile like a lift.

I'm Special
by Carissa Lewis

I see people here and there,
I see people everywhere.
Many of them have great jobs.
But me? No! I'm stuck in sobs.
When I was young, my mom would say,
"You are special, just in different ways."
But I would never believe her,
For right now, I'm stuck in my zipper.
One day when going to the mall,
I caught a glimpse of a waterfall.
It was tall, amusing, and a glittery blue.
I realized then I'm special too!
For when I passed that great big thing,
I realized I could sing!
Amazing music was coming from my voice!
So I sung a song of great rejoice.

Nature
by Avi Patel

Nature is the beauty of this planet,
It is leaves and trees and bees and hornets
Nature is fish and bears and plants,
Also the rainforests and bugs and ants
I like nature for it is calming,
A world full of interesting places and farming
The deep, dark seas and the brilliant heights,
A world full of nations and stars so bright
From Mount Everest in Nepal,
To Death Valley and the Panama Canal
The oceans and the continents,
The glaciers and the ice dents
Nature is great and astounding,
It is nature, just nature, but full of crowding
This is nature, a mysterious place,
Upon the Earth, a land of grace!

Rainy Days
by Teagan Grubb

Trees in the breeze are swaying in the air
Raindrops fall from the sky as we play inside
Grandma makes cookies while my brother and I play cards.

Friend
by Sunny Mann

Funny, playful
Caring, loving, affectionate
He's made for me
Buddy

Peace
by Tara Crowhurst

Nice, radiant
Loving, caring, respecting
Stopping wars on Earth
Happiness

Basketball Star
by Makenzie Goss

All of the basketball girls lined up.
Then the referee throws the ball
And they ...
Jump!
The girl gets it and ...
Scored!

Pecan Pie
by Tanner Flippo

The chewy sensation of pecan pie makes the day fly by the hours.
The sweet aroma is so strong, it makes you gasp for oxygen.
The top layer is rigid, and feels sticky like glue on rocks.
The pie is placed in the fiery pit to be cooked over the flame.
The brown coloring makes it look very tasty and delicious.
Ding! Goes the timer and the air is so thick, it hurts to breathe.

Flower
by Natalie Everett

Petals
Colorfully painted
They fill the Earth with color
As they bring spring in from winter

The Bear That Ate a Hair
by Donivan Echols

There was a bear that ate a hair.
He ran away to start the next day.
But got caught in a snare.

My Pants of Blue
by Pierre Domine

My name is Hugh.
My favorite color is blue.
I have some blue shoes, and some blue pants too.
I made my pants of glue.
It turns out that ants like sticky goo.
And so they ate my blue shoes, and my blue pants too.

The Months
by Wesley Ellis

In January and February you have to be bold
To go out into the bitter cold.
Now March and April, the start of spring
To sit on my porch on my comfy swing.
May and June in the hot summer days
When summer starts, you feel ablaze.
Into July and August you hear fireworks crack
As you feel the warm breeze upon your back.
Onto September and October, you have a scare
What stands on the back of your neck are little tiny hairs.
Finally November and December, the start of snow
You see it come down as it starts to blow.
Each month has its little special things
They all feel like little tiny kings.

The Season, Summer
by Eeshan Gurnani

Summer, the season when school is out,
All the children go running out to the public field,
To play their favorite and fun sport!
It's football, do you like that sport?
Summer is when it is really hot,
Hotter than spring, the season before summer.
Do you like summer? It's fun, right? Really fun!
I know other things about this wonderful and bright season!
Summer is a happy season, a favorite season
For some people like me and you!
Do you like seasons which are dull, dirty, not bright, and all gray
Like winter and fall? I would think no.
I like spring too.
The baby animals hatching,
The flowers starting to bloom,
Finally the sun shining on us!
Even if you disagree with what I am saying,
That is my descriptive and wonderful opinion about summer

Sun's Rays
by Nicholas Brophy

What is so bold
Creeping into places
And tiny spaces
Creating beautiful
Sights to behold ?
All day long it is so bright,
But only through the moon
Can you see it at night.
Through the clouds
In the sky it plays.
It never leaves
It always stays.
Oh yes, oh yes
It is the sun's rays!

Vets
by Emily Bradley

Vets help animals.
Big, skinny, tall, small
They help them all
Big or small

Stars
by Tristan Brass

Stars are similar to
Shooting, shining pictures of
Exploding fireworks in the sky.

My Hair's a Mess
by Grace Benda

My hair's a mess
I have to say
I really need a brush.
I heard a bird
Just lay a nest.
There are people that
Dance around in there,
That love my hair.
I say I need a rest
From my pesky, messy hair.

Friendship
by Sabrina Belden

Friendship is the most important thing
I'm so happy when I invite my friends over, then hear the doorbell ring
They make me laugh, they make me smile
I hope they stay for a while
"Come again," I say at the end of the day
So we can laugh and play, not only just today
Hurry back, see you soon
Maybe even tomorrow at noon
We could sing a song,
Or play ping pong
So please come over tomorrow
If not, my day will be filled with sorrow

Night
by Kylie Navarro and Cece Cannata

Thick layers of darkness,
Engulf me as I lay in bed,
I'm getting claustrophobic,
Dizzy in the head
A crack in the window,
Lets me see the dim, white moon,
A mysterious glowing sphere,
A shimmer of light,
On this icy, pitch black night
The dense and dark sky,
Morphs into a light blue height,
Happy to see a bright light,
The night is gone

Earth
by Olivia Mason

Everyone should have some green in them
Are you reducing, reusing, recycling?
Ready to help the planet stay green!
The planet will become greener than ever!
Having the best planet in the solar system: Earth!

Amelia Earhart
by Kristina Zakharchuk

Amelia Earhart was brave
Muriel once got stuck in a cave
Earhart, Amy was her mother
Little by little, she started flying farther
It took her a long time to cross the Atlantic Ocean
Amelia never married spoiled men

Everything was quite exciting
Amelia was scared, but she never stopped flying
Riches did not spoil her
However she loved beans
Amelia met two queens
Russell, Rosalind was being spied on by Earhart
Today even though Amelia Earhart died,
  –We still remember her and her kind heart.

Love
by Sammy Walsh

Love is in the air
Our love can create
Valentine's Day is filled with happiness
Each one of us can love

Hot
by Ibrahim Suid

Hot
Sweat, fire
Heat wave, droughts, rotten
Burning, sweating, falling
Blizzard
Icing, snowing, ice storm
Snow, cold
Freezing

For All The Hard Work My Parents Did
by Jeffrey Yin

For all the hard work my parents did,
I learn so much in one day,
Mostly when I'm a kid,
But they don't work for a pay.
When my parents play with me,
I get to have fun,
But when I get a B,
My mom helps in the sun.

My Best Friend Charlotte
by Hannah Drake

We lope and gallop upon the wind,
I know I'll be with her until the end.
I feel like I'm flying through the air,
As her mane sticks up and her nostrils flair.
Sometimes she throws me upon the ground,
But I get back up and run around.
I trust her as much as she trusts me,
And when we're together I'm as happy as can be.

Japan
by Matthew Grossman

Japan is where tea ceremonies all began;
When the Japanese are sad their fire dragon is mad;
Japan has great paintings during the winter season;
But when it is spring nature rings;
When the animals are happy they run and play and laugh all day;
I love Japan and all its wonders.

No One Is Standing In My Way
by Mariyana Van Arsdale

No one is standing in my way
It's all up to me
No one is standing in my way
You'll see.
I can do it on my own
Just believe
I can do it on my own
You'll see.
It might take some time just to build up to the top
I can do it on my own
In my very own ways
Everyday.
No one is standing in my way
I can make it to the top!
Sometimes it's hard
But I'll never stop!

The Green Machine
by Anthony Morgan

Green machine helps us breathe
Green machine helps us eat
Green machine we can climb
Green machine we can smell
Green machine they can smell good
Green machine they can live in water
The green machine

3rd Place

Jennifer Bowles

Jennifer wrote to us from the fourth grade
and made two things very clear.
She loves horses, and her brothers are very annoying.
Other than that, she enjoys life on her farm,
riding her horses, tending to the other animals
and playing with Mom, Dad, and yes, even her two brothers.

Morning In the Mountains
by Jennifer Bowles

As the sun leaps up onto the horizon,
The mountains yawn.
The trees
Stretch their branches.
The creeks
And streams
Fight the walls holding them captive.
And rays
Of light
Tip toe out of hiding.

2nd Place

Saffy Laurio

A true performer at heart,
when Saffy isn't writing poetry,
she's likely starring in one of her school's drama presentations.
In addition to being a proud member of the Girl Scouts,
she spends much of her free time swimming and playing the guitar.
Thanks for a lovely poem, Saffy.

Just Like the Wind
by Saffy Laurio

Just like the wind, I want to be,
Flowing between each and every tree.
And cooling little children on a hot summer day,
As well as seeing them laugh and play.
When I look up I see the sun and clouds.
But if I look down I see my shadow dancing along the ground.
I can fly so high in the sky, people seem like ants;
And so low, I see every little detail of every living plant.
Just like the wind, I want to be playful and free
And happy as a child could ever be.

1st Place

Callie Gudmonson

Callie submitted her poem to the America Library of Poetry
while in the fifth grade.
She is an avid reader and enjoys playing the piano and alto saxophone.
Her interests also include sports
and she loves competing in volleyball, basketball, and racing.
Her love of nature inspired her
to write this wonderfully descriptive piece
on the tranquility
of one of her favorite places.

The Forest
by Callie Gudmonson

In a forest
Beneath the tree
An ecosystem lives happily
Spiders spin webs
True and free
Birds sing their songs
Beautifully
Squirrels gather acorns carefully
And lay them in the old, old tree
Everything is done peacefully
In the forest
Beneath the tree

Division II

Grades 6-7

The Signs of Goodbye
by Cole Martinez

I see the smile pass your lips,
I touch you with my fingertips
I get goosebumps when you're here with me,
While I watch, your hair floats in the breeze
I really wish that you could stay,
So you won't have to go away
It seems that almost every day
You always try to slip away
Is there another besides me,
Or is it that you want to be free?
If this is why you want to leave,
I'll give you a little room to breathe
I thought we'd be together till the end,
But you think I'm just a friend
I always wanted you in my heart,
Now we're slowly drifting apart
My eyes fill with tears,
Which unlocks my deepest fears
Without you, I cannot fly,
I wish I would have found the signs of goodbye

Wind-Up Toy
by Crissy Gomez-Taylor

I am a wind-up toy being wound up by other people.
They wind me and wind me.
I march the way they want me to march.
I follow their every command, being pushed,
Pushed toward their towering expectations.
But, what if one day I break?
What if I crack?
What if I don't march the way they want me to march?
Or don't follow their every command?
Will they still love me?
Will they still play with me?
Or will I be thrown into a dusty old box of forgotten memories and broken dreams?
I am a wind-up toy.
And I must never break.

It's Snowin'
by Brenna Arnold

It's snowin'
Hey, it's snowin'
And the wind is a blowin'
The people on the street
Pass by for me to meet
They're snow covered
Hats and scarves and gloves covered
My mom makes hot chocolate
The kind I like a lot
The children of the avenue
Are building snowmen for me and you
It's snowin'
Hey, it's snowin'
And the wind keeps blowin'

Pride In America
by Victoria Coleman

In America one has the right to do many things.
One has the right to be free.
One has the right to speak freely.
One has the right to work hard and be anything they want to be.
In America one has the right to do many things.
In America there are many people from many different backgrounds.
One can be from any religion or any race.
One can be rich, poor, or "in between."
One can be from the city, the country, or the suburbs.
In America there are many different people from many different backgrounds.
In America one can become anything they want to be.
One can be a doctor, a lawyer, or a teacher.
One can be a fireman, a policeman, or a cashier.
One can be a dancer, a social worker, or even the president.
In America these are just a few jobs one can be.
America is a nation full of pride.
America is a nation full of ideals.
America is a nation full of opportunities.
America is a country based on hard work and dreams.

The Predator
by Haley Johnson

The lion is strong,
Power built in its long legs.
A bite force unmatched,
The ultimate predator.
It stalks in the tall grasses,
Silently watches and waits.
Something passes by,
The warm scent fills his nostrils.
His heart speeds faster,
Muscles tensing for the pounce.
Anxiety comes,
It can't wait any longer.
He bursts forward now,
Exhilarated with drive,
Drive to fill hunger.
The prey can't run anymore,
The victim goes down,
Feeling the fangs in its throat.
Its breath gets slower,
The lion has won the fight.

A Roller Coaster
by Jonathan Sledge

Life is a roller coaster
Going up and going back down
Is your life like a roller coaster?
Are you hiding a big fat frown?
Sometimes you'll win a medal
Sometimes you'll lose a friend
Your heart is now broken
It's desperately in need of a mend
You'll come across a new day
No longer are you blue
You'll meet a great new person
Your heart is now renewed
My life is like a roller coaster,
But I'm learning just how to ride
So far, it's been great fun
I'm striving for the "up" side

Tears of Dark Joy
by Chassity White

There are times when some fall down,
But great, loving, caring people are found.
We fall, we cry.
We always ask ourselves why.
We forget, we forgive.
But we all have trouble trying to live.
No life, no smiles.
There is something about love that is worthwhile.
Something that makes you cry and think,
If I had love my life wouldn't stink.
My sky is stormy,
But there is something that tells me,
True love is coming.
My crying, my forgetting, and worrying shall be no more.
Because my tears shall no longer be tears of dark joy.

Night Arrives
by Abhiram Lyer

Every night the lights turn out
There is quiet all about
Some are softly sleeping
Some are jubilantly leaping
Some are watching TV
Some, to stay awake, are drinking tea
Others are doing their work
The rest, with tons of work, shirk
Some think they can stay up late
By sleeping late, some observe their morning's fate
Some climb to bed
Their pillow, right beneath their head
Some are softly sleeping
Some are jubilantly leaping
There is quiet all about
Every night when the lights turn out

A Walk On the Beach
by Jillian Rohleder

The sun was setting
The sea was sparkling
The sound of the waves
Crashing on the beach
The seals barking
To the seagulls overhead
The seashells were shining
The sand was perfectly soft
On the soles of my feet
I sat perfectly still
To watch the playful sea
The new baby turtles begging to walk
The sea urchins being caught
The fishermen catching giant fish
The magnificent sunset

An Angel's Message
by Tylor Perry

An angel's message sent from above,
Consisting of warning, consisting of love
An angel's light helps you from sin
The message is not read, it comes from within
Love from many is sent to the few
If you are lucky a loved one will send a message to you
From a loved one that you lost,
The message comes without a cost
There is endless love in the message from an angel,
You are away from pain and for that I am thankful
The message sent means a lot,
It will let the pain stop
I lost the one most close to me;
I always thought our love could never be
You sent me a message and it set me straight
I am happy knowing you are past the heavens and the golden gate
I know these things because deep in my heart,
My mother sent me a message from deep in her heart

Spread Your Wings
by Carley Chicas

If you spread your wings
You will be able to go to college and leave,
But if you don't,
You will stay home your whole life
So just spread your wings
And go fly around this world

Abbey
by Krenda DeBoer

Holding my sister's neck ...
Screaming my name ...
Breeze hitting my cheeks ...
Something is wrong ...
Help ...

Remembering You, Father
by Lynette Chen

Mother says you were always kind;
An honest, ethical man;
A loving, caring father.
But all I have of you is mere imagination:
Since you left me at the tender age of one, I will never truly know you.
Father, you're like the missing piece–
The piece from the puzzle of my life,
The piece which can never be found.
Despite the distance between us, Father,
You are still my heart's pride. Mother always speaks highly of you.
The time you went through rigorous FBI training,
The time you represented your country to America,
Will always be your proudest moments, and mine.
What a loss to your country
When you died in 1997, before coming to America.
How everyone missed you!
You even made it to the newspaper;
The clippings honor you forever.
You will eternally be my father,
No matter where you are. I will always love you.

Young Money
by Dartravis McGee

Young money is the best.
They never rest.
They stay fresh from their head to ankles.
They be on the track like sprankles
They don't do drugs.
They have peace.
And they show love.
They don't act mean.
They have passed all the test.
They call T-Rex and make a mess.
They do things because they must.
As a group they know to have trust.
No ceiling

Scents of My Life
by Jamesa Easter

Some scents remind me of things in my life
Such as vanilla scents remind me of family
The sweet sensation makes me think of old times
Hanging out with aunts, uncles, and everyone else
Raspberry scents remind me of love
The love I get, have, and give
Citrus scents remind me of friends
How they make me feel good inside
And how we're so close that we're like a family
Lavender scents remind me of all the days,
All the days in the year and years to come
The days the sun shines bright and the birds sing
Strawberry scents remind me of everything fun
The funny jokes someone tells and how hard I laugh
The fun I have, like tickling or playing
While cinnamon reminds me of home
This particular scent brings back memories
Memories of growing up, having good times, and loving every moment

Seasons
by Tori Walker

Seasons come and go away.
Why can't they just stay?
When winter is here, autumn is gone.
Spring is here, winter has left.
Soon summer will come.
Spring stay, don't go away.
Another day passing away
Making it closer to a hot summer day
Closer and closer, here it comes
Spring is almost done.
Summer must come.
Kids jumping up and down with lots of reason,
It's almost the end of the season.

Countless Rose Buds
by Michael Pesola

Countless rose buds
Thus, merely one will endure
This one is favored.

Fun Under the Sun
by Megan Kumar Omelian

The days are so long, but it makes the nights so short
A time when there are parties every night of all sorts
Every girl and boy makes merry at the beach
Many enjoy that there are no teachers to teach
Families love to go out and have fun
But they hate it when the day is done
No one is stressed about a hard, complex test
It is more like they have only the feeling of zest
Even though it only lasts awhile
On every face there is a huge smile
And when running around brings a ligament tear
The beautiful weather makes one feel free of care
Summer stays with us only part of the year
It is a season filled with the sweet promise of cheer
I wish this could happen every day
But alas, everyone knows that summer won't stay

Music: the Love of Our Land
by Audra Beneux

Feel the rhythm,
Feel the beat.
That's why we're just so elite
Rocking it out down in the street
Make sure you feel it in your feet
Do the Macarena.
Do the Slide.
Make it spread out nationwide
That's why we dance side by side
That's why we dance far and wide
Hear the saxophone.
Hear the stereo.
It sets our faces all aglow
Ready, set, go!
Go with the flow
Feel the pizzazz.
Feel the demand.
That's why we stand
For the love of our land
I just hope you understand

One Little Poem
by Aly Reynolds

One little poem
Just a few little words
All coming together
Can mean so much
While one long poem
Can mean so little
Short phrases can say so much
Gray, gloomy days
Or sunny, happy mornings
Can share so much
While some phrases
Can be so long and boring
And big, long words
In big, long poems mean nothing
But, this is just one little poem
With little phrases
And little words
This is my poem!

Cats and Dogs
by Jack Freeland

A cat will sleep on your bed
A dog will drool all over its head
While dogs play fetch
Cats will do a giant stretch
Since time was made
Cats and dogs have usually obeyed
When a cat chases a mouse
A dog will chase a mailman around your house
Yeah, dogs are neat
However, cats are so sweet

Something About Love
by Haley McCoy

When love crashes
It opens a door
And he is
Out of sight
Out of sound
Out of mind
Out of love
And now she is independent

The Dreamer
by Victoria Morad

As I lay my head on my pillow
I do not shout, for I am very mellow.
I close my eyes to go to sleep,
But I hear a peep.
But now I know for I am in my dream world.
My own world;
It is amazing what my imagination can make.
For I can be anything even a baker that can make a cake.
I can drink all the Mountain Dew I want,
But I will not taunt the little creatures that live in my world,
For they are a great feature to have in the school of teachers.
But when I open my eyes I'm in reality where everything makes sense
And is intense

The Thing
by Cameron Fontaine

I run quick and fast
The creature is after me
I run to my house
I quickly race upstairs
I close the large door
I breathe heavily and stare
The thing is outside
It bangs loudly on my door
It is in the house
I look frantically for some way out of the room
There must be a way
The door will not hold for long
Aha! The attic
I climb just as the door breaks
I look down and gasp
All it is is a puppy
I stare awkwardly
I blink and look at the dog
I fall down and faint

Happy People
by Jamie McFerran

People should be happy
Instead of very scared,
And you should not be scared,
I'm a happy troll
And if you're not happy like a troll,
I will find you and cheer you up,
Or you could eat some icing,
Because it cheers you up.
Just like me,
If you don't like it then you're just weird,
You could also need some chocolate.
If you don't like it then too bad.
You may need some sugar,
It always helps
Or a playful puppy,
They will cheer you greatly.

Close To the Edge
by Kaleigh Stone

I'm too close to the edge
It's getting dark out and I'm scared
I have no where to go, no one to call, and no food
It's really cold out now,
And it's gotten even darker than before, and I can't see anything
It feels like my eyes have been sewn shut
Ouch! I ran into a tree
All of a sudden I see car lights
The car stopped and out came an old, wrinkly man
Wondering why I was wandering on the street on my own
After that he got back into his car and drove off

Spring
by Dylan White

Spring is amazing, the earth changes.
God starts ...
Popping the green above the white,
Blooming the blossoms,
Sparkling the fresh morning dew,
Painting the deep blue sky,
Fluffing the puffy white clouds,
Cueing the beautiful song birds,
And warming the breeze.
People start ...
Chopping their pants,
Cutting their sleeves,
Storing their coats for a long time,
And start drinking lemonade instead of hot cocoa.
Animals start ...
Waking up from their long winter nap,
And eating tons of food.
Spring is the most beautiful time of the year.

A Shark Was Ready To Eat
by Nimesh Poudel

A shark was ready to eat,
It really wanted some meat,
So it caught some small fish,
Put them on a small dish,
And ate without taking a seat.

Sisters
by Ashley Brooks

Sarah, my sister, makes me feel useless
She tells me to move without being polite
She leaves me out of everything
If I get two miles within her bubble,
She screams and moves away
Sometimes she doesn't consider my feelings
Sisters can be a wonderful thing, but not mine
Sarah doesn't listen to me at all
She always thinks I'm giving her lectures
Sometimes, I am so mad, I want to hit her
If I do, she'll tell Mom and I'll get in trouble
If I get a good grade and tell Mom,
She says, "Wow!" in a sarcastic tone
She won't lift a hand to play with me
She embarrasses me when I don't deserve it,
But sometimes I just have to remember that she is my sister
And sisters annoy each other

Nature
by Nicholas Gregory

The roar of the sea, the whoosh of the forest
And the boom of thunder, and the sprinkle of rain,
The whirl of the wind,
Sounds of nature are the best,
An alarm is unnecessary when you have nature
You wake up to the chirp-chirp of birds,
The bark of the dog, the whirl of the wind,
I love nature

Peace
by Juliette Klassen

Peace is our ally
Words against words should be fought
Violence do not

Night Sky
by Shreya Sudarshana

The silence.
The stillness.
The dark sky.
The twinkling.
The brightness.
The stars up so high.

The Moon
by Alex Warner

How bright your reflection,
It lights your way through the darkness.
You are a beautiful object in the sky,
You, oh, Moon, control life on this planet;
And it is irresistible not to stare at such a beauty!

I Miss You
by Zoey Carter

I miss you and your kindness–
Maybe it's your kind voice–
I love you
So sad–so sad
You're awesome and I miss you;
Only your voice comforts me
You are still in my heart

Winter
by Shreyan Jain

When the lush green grass cowers under a blanket of snow,
And the world turns white like in the movie "8 Below,"
When the frequent blackouts interrupt your favorite TV show,
That's when you know it's winter.
When children go out and have a great big snowball fight,
And you see kids sledding left and right,
When children stay outside until they get frostbite,
That's when you know it's winter.
When the fields are adorned with snow angels and snowmen,
And baby bear cubs are born in the den,
When the church bells sing like the music from Heaven,
That's when you know it's winter.
When you go to parties that last all night,
And the joy of giving gifts makes the world festive and bright,
When there isn't a single unhappy soul in sight,
That's when you know it's winter.

The Chasing
by Emma Styers

Her feet pounding against the forest floor
Her chest about to burst
And her muscles rippling under her coat
She chased the antelope
Through the trees
Under the canopy
Out of the forest.

Your Imagination
by Luka Ivandic

In the middle of Africa,
At places still unknown to man,
There are many animals thought dead.
Mammoths, dodo birds and saber-tooth tigers
All rule the land,
In a place usually called your imagination.

Cheerleading
by Abby Hanlon

Cheerleading, a fun exciting explosion in your heart.
Jumps in the air.
Tumbling here and there.
Dancing everywhere.
Cheering loud and clear.
I love to cheer!

If ...
by Meredith Adcock

If people cared, I wouldn't be able to see through the top of the trees,
The water would be clean enough to swim in,
City air would be as clean as country air
If people cared, the endangered wildlife would have more spaces,
Preservation grants would have more funding,
People would want to volunteer to help
If people cared, if people cared

I Live In a Bubble
by Brittany Belanger

I live in a bubble
Floating around without touching anything, glistening in the sun
And the world around me is beautiful and big
In my own confined space,
I am in a world of my own,
Waiting for someone to pop my bubble

Kitty-Cat
by Hannah Frame

Her purr sounds like the sun rays hitting the ground.
Her paws are like little clouds coming down.
Her orange fur is like honey drizzling off a waterfall.
Her eyes reflect her personality.
Her nose is like a spot of pink cotton candy.
When she comes to cuddle me, it feels there is no place I'd rather be.
The one I am addressing is my cat, Honey.

America
by Kyle Hixon

America is special to me because I have freedom and rights
They let me be the best I can.
America is my country
That is why America is special to me.

McDonald's Burn
by Brian Wratten

Fatty don't worry
I bought a McFlurry
They sell soda
As green as Yoda
6 in Lodi
Make you die
Big Mac fatty
Yo' tummy flabby
Be concerned
'Cause the Quarter Pounder's returned
Fatty be craving
Others be plain
(Plain fat)
McDonald's Burn

The Crazy Life
by Skyler Wilson

As I'm sitting in my house
I begin to think of that mouse
I'm sitting in this rocking chair
Thinking about Ric Flair
I get up from my chair
And look up into the air
I begin to look downward
And turn into a coward
If only I knew how to play guitar
I wouldn't be working in this bar
And now you know how my life is
I wonder where that mouse lives

Free
by Shannon Hewlett

Autumn is in the air, and it is raining leaves.
I feel my hair blowing in my face
And I can smell the flowers.
I'm in a field, full of mustard flowers
And it's like I'm in a perfect dream.
I tap my heels and now there is thunder.
I feel my horse's hair whip in my face
And his easy breath as Marby gallops across the field.
The sound of his hooves are powerful but sure.
Now, as I open my eyes, I feel wonderful.
Wonderful and without a doubt, free.

Scary House
by Hope Zollars

Walk into the scary house
Creaking floorboards, bleak cobwebs
No one will
Be seen
Again

In Dreams
by Michael Lowry

In dreams you can do anything, be anyone, see everything.
In dreams it is a world all to your seeing.
Imagine, just imagine, a world of your own, it's all yours ...
In dreams it can be quiet, but suddenly the silence is broken, you have awoken.
Now we wait for next time, for the next ... dream.
The day goes fast, almost like you can't remember the past,
It's gone, you're back in your other life, starting a new day in your quiet world ...
But it isn't the same, it's dark, abandoned, trees are falling, animals are crying,
The Earth is dying, the air is polluted, it is hard to breathe, cars are honking,
It is hot, but the sun is hidden ...
I am in the future, I thought
Now I realize how much we are killing our Earth ... Our home ... Ourselves.

Night
by James Sousa

Noises on the window.
Roars from the bed.
Steps in the hallway.
Monsters on the ground.
Creeps in the closet.
Yelling from the yard.
Turn on the lights
And no one's there.

Mommy
by Sydney Cooper

"Mommy, Mommy," cried a child so small
"I need a hug!"
"Mommy, Mommy," the child yelled
"Can I have a kiss, please?"
"Mommy, Mommy," the child cried
"Lay with me, please. and Mommy,
I love you!"

When You Say ...
by Sandra Walle

You said you would be there when I fell ... Why am I still on the ground?
You said you would dry my tears ... Why am I still crying?
You said you would help me get through the pain ... Why am I still hurting?
You said you would be my light ... then why am I wandering in darkness?
You said you would be there ... Where are you now?
It feels like something is missing when you're gone.
But when you're here, it's like darkness has swept the land
I don't want to let you go, but if you're only going to let me down
I guess it would be best if you go
All you do is bring pain
You've made many promises that you've never kept
You say you're sorry but we both know you're not
I always gave you chances, but you never came around.
Although you've caused me lots of pain, I thank you in a way
'Cause you have made me stronger.
Now I know when to say "You're not sorry"
Now I know when to say "It's done"
Now I know how to say "Get lost"
Now I know how to say ... "It's over!"

The Family That Prays
by Barbara Coward

My family prays
My family cries
Wondering why
Some people had to die
Or wondering why
Our dad had to go
But what we do know
Is that God said let it be so
We pray
We sing
Knowing that it is the right thing
Praising God for what he has done
Like giving up His only Son
Oh thank you, Jesus
Yes, Lord
Are the words that we say
When giving thanks,
When we all pray

Snow
by Briana Balladares

Snow is a white blanket
Over the cold ground
Looking for someone
To freeze
Again.

Peace and Serenity With Nature and the Seasons
by Kristina Furtado

Chirp, chirp
The birds are calling
The leaves are falling
The flowers are bright
Like the sun, what a sight
The clouds are out
And the animals are about
These are the signs of March, April, and May
Summer is also on its way

Disneyland
by Angel Garcia

My first time at Disneyland, it was fun
My dad was happy to meet Mickey Mouse
When it got dark everybody was done
In the hotel it looked like a huge house
On the second day it was really bright
I went on a ride, I got really scared
The roller coaster was really tight that night
I had a sandwich and found a small hair
On the last day, my parents and I walked
My parents saw a Mickey Mouse blue ball
My mom saw a Goofy toy that could talk
We saw Goofy and he was really tall
And we went to a huge Disneyland parade
And that parade, my parents said, "Hurray"

Pride In America
by Anastasia Anderson

Where is your pride?
Pride for America of course,
Think about the people who died,
And fought for our American force.
It's called the land of the free,
Because everyone is treated in a fair way
And we have plenty of rights, you can see,
There's a mix of cultures, let's say.
An American can be any religion,
They could be any race,
An American can make their own decisions,
And have their personal space.
Whenever something has brought us sadness,
They have still failed,
Our spirit and hope is simply endless,
It will never be bailed.
From west to east,
And north to south,
You may find peace,
And speak words from your own mouth.

Spring
by Mounika Narayanan

Spring is the time of year
When flowers start to bloom.
As they begin to reappear,
They illuminate the entire room.
Spring is the time of year
When children play all day.
But even though night is near,
They sing, slide, and skip away.
Spring is the time of year
When skies cry down raindrops.
"Drip drop drip," I hear,
As it rains from here to distant hilltops.
Spring is the time of year
When nature is in constant change.
Like the movement of the clock right here,
The cycle of life begins to rearrange.

The Forever Horse
by Darian Dyer

Could anything so beautiful
Have been put on this world?
A dream we dream
In a lovely illusion
He nickers,
He neighs
It's like he's writing a symphony, for my ears only
Like bells ringing on the gusty wind
He bucks,
He kicks
His fine muscles ripple under his gleaming coat
Radiant colors, imaginative patterns
He collects his canter
He extends his trot
He comes gaited, he comes swift
His presence is not easily ignored.
He tosses his mane in joy
He swishes his tail in frustration
He is God's gift, so we can be happy
He is the Forever Horse.

Summary
by Monique Hung

To me, summer is like a tool
That helps me escape from school
That enables me to sit on a grassy hillside all day long
With my ears open to a beautiful, brilliant bird song
Summer is the season in which all fruits are at their ripest
They are ready to be picked from their leafy, green trees
The meadow is dappled with flying from flower to flower bees
Whose glossy, glimmering, golden honey is at its sweetest
Going to the beach is the best way to spend a hot summer's day
For that's where white seagulls and snappy hermit crabs play
I'd like to surf on the ocean's roaring waves,
And later on explore the nearby, but spooky, caves
I have more time to do the things that I want during summer
Like going shopping with my friends at the mall
However, I find it kind of a bummer
That summer has to end and I will have to go back to school in the fall

Our Melting Snowman
by Anusha Sundar

Trickling down, dropping in the deep snow,
I watch the clouds' tears as cold as ice go.
Crunching and crackling the white bed,
I rush to build a snowman ahead
My little friends and I built up till the nose,
And skipped all around our snowman that froze
Joy and glee filled the winter air,
Because for our snowman we showed love and care
But when he started frowning, we knew,
That winter's joy would only last for a few,
Our snowy man started dripping into the snow,
And none of us knew where he would go
Although my friends and I missed the man of snow,
We knew we had to learn to let go
But where the snowman had left us alone,
A little, glowing, green sprout had grown

Spring
by Nihar Wahal

Red roses rise tall and high;
The bees, making honey, give a sigh;
The seeds from the flowers drop by;
Spring has come far and wide.
All the little kids run outside;
Playing their games of seek and hide;
Tossing the football and "going wide;"
Why not, wouldn't you do the same?
The little animals in the wood came
Outside, and took some fame.
All gathered together in the same
Place to gain our admiration.
The animals will eventually stun
Us, with their grace, like the sun.
But divine will only be one
The spirit of spring.

Fall
by Kriti Sharma

Softly the leaves tread on the ground,
Golden and glittering sound all around.
Gently they fall into a mound.
Fall is the season of autumn.
The plants are now at their ripest.
To pick them now for winter is best.
Fruit pies and salads to feed our guests.
Fall is the harvest time of the year.
School starts for all the children.
To learn many new things makes them grin.
An apple for the teacher again.
Fall is the season for school.
The sun shines brightly on our faces,
Leaving summer behind without any traces.
Flowers, quietly as mice, droop in their vases,
Fall is the most peaceful season of all.

Fickle Clouds
by Brittney Thornton

The clumsy clouds once reached down to me
To share some frosty fluff
I tried to give it back to them
For I was cold enough
But they misread my actions
And sent down shards of ice
Which I did swiftly dodge
In this freezing paradise
The next day the clouds curled their lips
And hissed and snarled in anger
And flicked out their spiteful yellow tongues
Under them I was too frightened to linger
But soon they silently slithered away
The sky again bright and blue
And left behind were little vines
And fabulous flowers, too

Winter
by Ganesh Tulshibagwale

Winter is a time with cheer,
Christmas, family, and root beer.
The wailing wind will wonder why
People do not fear its war cry.
In the hills I think I see
People hurtling down on skis.
Like a rocket they speed downwards,
Kenneth, Peter, Judy, and Howard.
And when the snowstorms whirl with white,
We sit gathered around the firelight.
The blizzards outside may rant and roar,
But we are protected behind our mighty door.
The writers of old are so very wrong
In vilifying winter in poem and song.
They seem to think that winter and death
Should always be said together in the very same breath.

Give Me One Answer
by Sidney Bryant

Is there a good song?
Tell me I'm not wrong.
Are you sick?
You look like a stick.
Is it loud?
I wish I were on a cloud.
Do you want to scream?
I hope this is a dream.
Are we in a park?
It's so dark.
Are you a moon?
You look like a balloon.
Are you a toy?
You seem like a boy.
Do you want school to end?
You want to get to see your friend.
Can you say hi?
Come on, it's easy as pie.
Did you say your name is Kidney?
My name is Sidney.

The Seasons of the Year
by Nicole Deacon

In the wonderland,
People walking hand in hand.
Skating on the frozen pond;
Decorating the conifer fronds.
Spring leaves are a lime green.
Cute little birds are sure to be seen.
The clear blue sky lets in the light
Of the sun shining oh, so bright.
School's out! Let's scream and shout!
Fun's what it's all about.
Spending the day at the pool,
Just trying to stay cool.
The most beautiful season of all.
Harvest the crops in the fall.
The wind howls like wolves to the moon.
While winter wonders are coming soon.

Gift For My Friend
by Rohan Dhoopar

I went to buy gifts for my friend.
I searched the store from start to end.
Although I searched so very hard,
I had to buy him a gift card.

The Gifted Tree
by Helen Chen

On the tree was a star, which shone bright in the light,
Underneath was a present, which might be a kite.
It was shaped like a diamond and wrapped up with care.
I would open it, but I would not really dare.
I should wait until Christmas like how I should do.
But too bad, I have already taken it to my playpeno.

Wonderful Winter
by Ithika Mirji

In winter, in winter,
The trees put on a coat.
This is what we all note.
The plants began to cripple,
Like shirts getting little.
In winter, in winter,
Animals eat their scrumptious food
In a happy and cheerful mood.
Some animals start to hibernate
With their loveable mate.
In winter, in winter,
People start to get warm
By staying in bed and ignoring their alarm.
Though others like to go for a walk,
And while they are at it, they like to talk.
In winter, in winter,
The time of joy and pleasure remains, Christmas
Where we sometimes under mistletoe, give each other a kiss.
Then there are always the gifts,
Which can always give a child's spirit a lift.

The Circle of Seasons
by Adham Kamel

Summer, summer, summer is here.
There won't be any tears
From school and homework.
The sun is shining like
A fluorescent night-light.
Fall, fall, fall is here.
The leaves fall from a tree
Like good hot coffee
Spilling on the dirty old floor.
Winter, winter, winter is here.
People want to play
In a snowy Christmas Day.
Bells everywhere are sounding,
Ring-ring-ding-ding.
Spring, spring, spring is here.
Flowers are blooming.
Like a little child growing up
Then we start
All over again.

A Season To Come
by Adeel Khan

Winter you cover the world in snow, you grasp the world in your cold icy hands
You turn fertile land into barren wastelands
The bears are in hibernation all around the nation
The world is in isolation
The green grass has turned to white
The white is now the only sight
It makes me feel lonely
When the world is icy
Then comes spring which always sings
It sings a song about living
Birds, flowers, and butterflies are born again
To set the world on its feet again
When it's spring I always sing
About how to be a king
I am always happy on this day
For every day is my favorite day

Winter
by Durga Ganesh

Winter, winter, I know why you bring
Merry winds that sweetly sing
To shivering people very bored
Of the chilly weather, oh, so cold!
Winter, winter, I know why you bring
Snowflakes falling down with a ring,
And landing softly on my head
Oh, this is as soft as white bread!
Winter, winter, I know why you bring
Furry cats playing with string
While mothers are happily at work,
Sewing mittens with special patchwork!
Winter, winter, I know why you bring
All these wonders before the coming of spring,
For all of existence should be ready
To welcome new life with nature's confetti!

Grief
by Emma Levine

Grief is the sorrow that holds you back.
He is small and unnoticed for now.
But when somebody is sick or passes away,
He transformed into something big and powerful.
Like a raging tiger.
He sweeps you away into a deep dark cage distress.
As you sit into the little corner of that cave
Through the only little hole in the top of the cave
You see grief sweep over the world,
Looking for people like you to bring into the hiding places of their mind.
As he does that he brings a blanket of blackness that chases after him.
Only the little sparks of hope flicker out of that blanket of black.
But not only are you punished by him, he is punished by himself.
He is cursed with being immortal, to have to live with himself.

Gone
by Jasmine Goldsberry

A painful remorse burdens aching souls
A hole in the heart, irreplaceable
All that was left were the flickering coals
In the dead of the night, and susceptible
An icy wind blew, and swept him away
As the hour hand struck on the cold midnight
His soul has departed, it pains to say
Stuck in the midst of a hazy twilight

The Magnificent Gift
by Sonia Varandani

I saw my present with alarm
And saw a gorgeous little charm
A tear escaped me in my joy
I had not got a single toy!

Sock Puppet
by Allie Denton

I guess God does this to help me
To show me how everything rolls
It is just I look up into his eyes and smile,
He doesn't even know.
I want his hand in mine
And another of his kind.
He breaks my heart, then calls me up on the phone
And says, "I want you as my own."
He tears me down, then pulls me right back up,
Like a sock puppet, he can only stop
But will he? Will he ever stop?
Stealing my heart, then throwing it right back at me
Like a dagger to my heart. Am I that vulnerable?
Or am I vulnerable for him because it is meant to be,
Just not yet?

Best Friends
by Janella Margarita Pecson Juan

Everyone knows us
We're a group of friends
We make mistakes but never fuss
Together we have hearts to mend
We hang out all the time
I wouldn't trade you for a nickel nor dime,
I am always counting on you
And do best at what you do
If one fails, we all fail
We hug when one breaks a nail
We annoy each other
And we put up with one another,
We're random and crazy
Or just sometimes lazy
We fight over something stupid
Like believing in Cupid,
But this is the best I could ever get
Because you guys are the best girls I ever met
So forever shall we stay, BFF's till this day

The Endless Cycle
by Geet Bhade

The tree is barren and robbed of its life
The river is hidden by frost
The meadow is empty, its beauty has gone
Winter brings death to the world
The tree is filling now, the leaves as sharp as a knife
The river is flowing fast, the ice is lost
The meadow shows beautiful blooming blossoms, nature's phenomenon
Spring brings a rebirth to the world
Now the tree is heavy with fruit, calling to children, a fife
The river is at its peak, with fish embossed
Our fellow meadow is alive with animals, bustling with life even before dawn
Summer brings growth to the world
Our beautiful tree has turned crimson; the color of the fallen's blood after strife
The high–spirited river is slowing now, life taking its cost
And finally, our dear meadow's inhabitants are fading away
As winter's presence is made known, and the cycle goes on
Autumn brings a change to the world

Missing You
by Cori Jones

I've built up a wall
So you don't know
Of the feelings
I try not to show.
You are gone
But I'm still here,
What am I supposed to do
Without you near?
My life is filled with happiness
But with happiness comes sorrow,
People will be missed
But it's a new day tomorrow.
Life goes on
So I wake with a smile,
Telling the world
Everything's worthwhile.
In the end
I'll do what is right,
I'll never forget you
My laughter and light.

Ancient Village
by Violet Gorton

As I climb toward the moss covered rocks
I see an ancient village.
It's filled with glistening water
As the tomb brings hope.
I see the villagers coming
Down the charming trail with pots in their hands.
Their children run and laugh
While the parents are blessed.
The water is a lovely teal
Red, gold, and vivid fish float.
And as the waterfall runs through the village
It casts the hope of one day being immortal.
As I climb toward the moss covered rocks
I see an ancient village.

I Wish
by Alfredo Garcia

I wish everyone had a friend.
There are people sitting by themselves in the cold.
But if they were to have a friend they would not be alone.
There are people that have no friends,
Playing alone at the park or skipping rocks over water,
But if you had a friend the world would be better.
And there are people that are alone all the time and hate everything
But, if they had a friend they might just open their eyes,
And step out of the dark,
And just be saved,
From the curse that is loneliness.

Hummingbird
by Jessica Ervine

Graceful and simple and yet so complex.
Beautiful colors, delicate features, petite but fast.
No bigger than a water glass.
Hummingbird.

My Disney Vacation
by Ashlyn Lang

A magical place
Fireworks over the castle
Disney vacation

As the Wind Blows
by Dominick Elkins

The wind through the trees,
Like a simple summer's breeze
The trees shake as the wind blows,
But still all is quiet
As the wind blows and blows
The trees still shake
In a simple summer's breeze,
But peace means quiet
As quiet still means peace

Seed By Seed
by Tristan Arquitt

Seed by seed the flowers grow.
But then comes winter snow.
But then there is spring that makes everyone glee.
Don't you know God made this for you and me.
When they bloom they are the prettiest.
When you see them they look magnificent.
Just remember they will always be there.
Because that is where God made them for us to share.

Ice Cream
by Vinny Abdallah

Ice cream is good, ice cream is bad,
But you can always eat whatever you have.
Everyone loves it, including my dad.
Ice cream is good when you're sad.
There are thirty-one types at Baskin Robbins
So when you're chillin',
Come out and buy billions of ice cream.

Live Happy
by Jonathan Dinh

To smile with joy is to live with glee,
As to be sorrow is to be mournful,
To elate, the farthest one can be,
Only one man himself can be woeful
Depression will lead life out together
Laugh, and all the whole world laughs with you
To be sad will drop you like a feather,
Just a smile is all you have to do
Sing with passion and the nation will hear
Sigh and it will be lost in the air,
Cry with flooding tears and friends won't come near,
And all would shrink away from voicing care
So smile every minute of your life,
Or your happy life will be full of strife!

My Thoughts About Life
by Davaisse Davis

Life is a maze ... you gotta know when,
You gotta know why!
Life is not perfect.
You can think all you want,
Because everybody has ups and downs in their lives!
When you see or hear someone bragging about how good their life is going,
Go up to them and say, "Why?"
Why are you bragging about your good life,
When some people don't get what you get,
And go where you go,
And do what you do.
If they say not a word, walk away
And leave their life alone!

Song of the Starlings
by Violet Cole

A song rings in my ears,
I walk outside to hear it louder,
I look up,
Starlings are soaring through the sky
As swift as an arrow,
They dart upward,
And then down, staying in unison.
The melody of their quiet chirps is beautiful
And harmonizes with the soft, tinkling sound the wind makes.
The birds suddenly curve to one side and then the other,
An alive abstract painting before my eyes
As the paintbrush that leads them drops down,
The birds look at me,
Take pity on me, the poor human stuck on the ground,
But a look is enough,
My spirits begin to fly with them.
After a final note to their melody, a final stroke to the painting of the sky,
The starlings fall into the nearby bamboo,
And the song of silence penetrates my ears
Until the starlings sing again tomorrow.

Zane's Death
by Randi Clark

I think of you night and day,
Why you killed yourself
I can never figure it out
I always thought you were so happy with your life
I wish you would not have killed yourself.
So scared when I saw you hanging
I miss you so much
I miss your smile
I miss your hugs.
I miss how you would always be there
When I needed you.
The sweatshirt and picture are all I have left
I will keep the stuff you gave me safe
I will comfort your mom.
I must see you again
But I can't.

The Life of Cats
by Emery Brock

Alley cats roam streets
While house cats are in their sweets
Oh, the life of cats

The Graveyard
by Janie Browning

The graveyard is a sinister place
Filled with evil things
Creaking skeletons, misty ghosts
Vampires with mismatched wings
Demons hide behind gravestones
Grinning their awful grins
Souls of passed people
Tortured because of their sins
Bats circle the air, their screeches fill the night
Dead soldiers rise, swords clash in the fight
If I were to visit the graveyard, I would choose a time that's best
Because I'd rather be in the graveyard when the creatures are at rest

Sonnet #13
by Christopher Bamber

There's a region in the Caribbean
Where people celebrate the sun and sand
It once was ruled by French and English men
The cane and coffee made it rich and grand
As Europe left this sparkling gem to die
The people multiply, the soil erodes
The earthquake there made the rich nations cry
From big nations to islands such as Rhodes
The brotherhood of man unites as one
Lending a helping hand to those in need
To raise some funds some people want to run
This charity increased, we plant a seed
Haiti encourages each man to act
The world is not perfect and that's a fact.

Monsters
by Tristan Moore

Monsters big
And monsters small,
Monsters short
And monsters tall,
Monsters scary
And monsters nice,
Monsters hairy
And monster lice,
Monsters sing
And monsters dance,
Monsters howl
And monsters prance.
All monsters are different
But why can't we treat them the same.
People are mean to monsters,
And that means that they are lame.

A Long, Long Time Ago
by Daric Echols

A long, long time ago
It was dark and cold,
People would wage war
And kill for nothing more,
Back then it was harsh
Like a crocodile-filled marsh,
But don't go back to misery
Let's not repeat history,
A long, long time ago
It was so horrible you know,
Many deaths during war
Because bombing planes would soar
Many days of misery
Followed this history,
A long, long time ago
It was dark and cold.

A Million Things
by Ciandra Oo

There lie a million things just right outside my door
And yet I'm warned repeatedly not to step a foot outside
Because there lies a million dangers just right outside my door
A million things I can't imagine
Beckoning and tempting me
To step outside and leave my shelter
To wander the world
And experience those million things
For being young and curious,
My hand reached tentatively for the handle,
To follow those encouraging whispers
Into a world of a million things
But another hand, warm and plump,
Took mine and a gentle voice scolded softly,
"There lie a million things just right outside that door.
But if you stay with me, you'll have twice of everything you'll ever have out there."
Peering upwards, I gaze into my mother's affectionate eyes,
And there I saw the love and life she was willing to offer for me,
I take her words and push myself into her reassuring hug
That is worth more than a million reasons to go outside that door.

Bloodlust
by Rachel Wallace

My eyes open
Today is the day of our first hunt.
I crouch in a field
A rabbit is only three yards ahead of me.
I spring but miss
It runs into a burrow.
I come home with nothing
My siblings laugh at me.
I keep trying.
I track a deer.
I find it.
I crouch low to the ground.
When I'm only a few feet away I spring.
It runs fast
But not fast enough
It's over.
Bloodlust is upon me.
I drag it home
To find my siblings' eyes wide with shock.
They never killed anything as big as a deer.

If Only One Time
by Meaghan McCoy

If only one time
I could really speak my mind
And just let my emotions flow
If only one time
I could tell him I loved him
And have him pull me into an eternal love
If only one time
I could steal my freedom
And forget the everlasting worries of life
But unless time stops, I'll never get my one time,
My one time to rebel,
My only chance to confess,
My one day to live
If only one time

I Can't
by Destini Still

I can't write a poem,
It's too hard
I don't know how to write,
There is too much noise,
My pencil is dulling,
My leg hurts,
Ouch,
I jammed my finger,
I'm tired,
I'm bored,
I want to play a game
Like basketball,
Soccer,
Or kick ball,
My leg hurts,
My back itches,
My head hurts,
I'm hungry
I can't, I can't, I can't
Hey, I just wrote a poem!

My Wretched Little Brother
by Alex Rossington

My wretched little brother is always such a bother.
Oh yes, he is my brother, the one who always annoys my father.
My mother thinks he is an angel
But if you see a boy with that much hair gel he could and can't be an angel.
Oh yes, you see that sweet little smile
But under that sweet little smile is dirty fingernails
And there is so much more that I could tell,
But I won't because there's just too much. My dear, wretched, little brother,
I hope you will grow out of this wretched little brother stage.
I hope you will or else I will have to lock you up in a cage.
So, wretched little brother, who annoys my father,
Who has a smile that makes our mother think you're an angel,
Yes, you, my wretched little bro', I really can't wait till you grow!

I Can See
by Blake Roark

I can see a bird up so high.
You need an airplane to get that high.
As I go up, I see it fly
And then it says hello, then goodbye

You Make Me Feel
by Etna Roman

Every time you gave me that look
I would get lost in your eyes.
Every time you gave me that smile
It made me feel a feeling that I never felt before.
Every time you would say all those sweet words to me
I would fall in love with you more and more each day.
Every time you called me your loser
I laughed and felt special to someone in so many ways.
Every time you hugged me when something was wrong
My problems fell apart and nothing could go wrong again.
Every moment I spent with you
Was like one of the happiest dreams ever.
Every time you gave me that kiss
I would always feel a twinkle in my stomach
As if a butterfly was flying in there.

Prose
by Sierra Pell

Page by page, a story unfolds.
Chapter by chapter, word by word
As I read, my mind travels to far off places.
The library, the place to read book after book, story after story.
After six or seven hours, I become tired of reading, pen and paper I seek.
For I read, I write.
I play music, I do math, I sing, I dance.
Day versus night, who will win?
Page by page, a poem, a prose will unfold.
The sweet smell of rose emanates from description.
From a poem, a book, a prose, a story, a novel
Comes knowledge, imagination, pure fun.
A person once told me, "The pen is mightier than the sword."

I Am
by Le'Aysha Pearson

I Am Le'Aysha Pearson
I am creative and beautiful
I wonder about what will happen in the future
I hear my family encouraging me and telling me I can do it
I see the truth even if it's hidden behind a mountain of lies
I want there to be peace, hope, love, and happiness for everyone
I am creative and beautiful
I pretend that there is a totally different world out there that we don't know about
I feel the warm embrace of my mother holding me close
I touch the hearts and souls of the people who need my help
I worry about the thousands of people being murdered and abused everyday
I cry tears of pain for the father I never knew
I am creative and beautiful
I understand that if you want change, you have to do something about it
I say that you can't let the fear of failing keep you from following your dreams
I dream that someday there will be world peace,
And all of the hate and anger will go away
I try to be the best that I can be
I hope that I will never be forgotten
And that I'll be remembered for making the world a better place
I am creative and beautiful

The Green Emerald
by Lauren Kafka

Can you hear me whistle in your ear?
I am headed for a world with no fear
Someplace dangerous, yet free,
Nothing but air and energy
Colors are beautiful, shadows are dark,
Dirt is rough like tree's bark
Creatures wander fast and silent,
Only sometimes are they violent
Vines are scattered, running wild
Flowers are pretty, very styled
Together they stand ...
The future looks grand
I am the wind and this is my emerald
I call it my forest, my ultimate playground
There is none other in the world,
Now my forest is calling, you can hear its sound.

All My Heart
by Ashley Rabenold

You've been with me throughout my whole life,
Through the good and the bad, when I was happy and sad.
Your kindness can never be repaid, your love can never be explained.
I love you more than 1 million flowers,
Each petal representing my feelings and dreams.
I love you more than 1 billion, 1 trillion or 1 zillion of anything.
I love you more than you could ever know, please don't ever go.
You are the only grandparents I have and I will never forget you!
All my love is like a glove, surrounding and keeping you warm.
You are truly amazing and my love for you is blazing.
I love you with all my heart!

Love
by Arianna Kelly

Is a beating heart
Is what parents give us
Is a red rose
Is a very long journey

God of War
by Kyle Payne

Being the God of War isn't bad,
When you're betrayed by your dad,
Especially if you're the God of War,
When you have Titans on your side
You can't be beat,
Even if your father is Zeus,
But he's white as a goose,
Even if it takes days to get to him,
You can always get there,
Especially if he is an old man and you're the God Of War,
He may have all of Olympus on his side,
But the Titans still tower over them.

Masquerade
by Rylie Munn

There is a time every year,
Whether you're near or far, all will hear.
It is a magnificent ball that takes place in the fall.
All can come like a prince or a maid
So put a mask upon your face and join the masquerade.
Now, some may dress as a valiant knight
While others mask as a queen in white.
There are so many colors through the night, like rose red to turquoise blue
Or maybe some chestnut or some burgundy, too!
So don't hide in the shade,
Step out and don't be afraid, and go join the masquerade.
You may see your dear friend or archenemy too,
Or maybe a duke from France and your old Auntie Sue.
You may see the Queen of England with her elegant and golden shine
Or maybe just your old town friend dressed quite fine.
You may see someone with pearl earrings or someone with some jade.
So put a mask upon your face and join the masquerade.

What Happened?
by Emily McClung

I didn't think it would end like this
We were just messing around
I didn't think it would end like this,
It all just fell to the ground
What happened?
What happened?
It wasn't supposed to be this way,
We weren't supposed to change it
But we did
Oh, yes we did
With all our unfortunate wit
We made new things that made it worse,
That we never should have made
The world was supposed to be a better place,
But we, the people, changed it

Road of Fear
by Rosa Lopez

As I walk the road of fear,
I search for answers far and near
I'm in a dark, cold place that I can't call home
But I'm going to let go of all pain and release myself
Before tomorrow becomes today
I'm ready to know what's ahead of me
And see the future as it appears

Basketball
by Ashlee Long

Basketball is like Christmas
Everybody loves it
There is no end
My shoes talk to me with every squeak
My heart is screaming with every breath
I can't believe the season is over

Daffodil Symphony
by Lily Maxfield

The daffodils are trumpets
That play the song of spring
They lift their bugles to the sky
And let their music ring
When spring herself comes trotting by
The daffodils reach to the sky
They sing their special song for her
But only in a murmur
If you listen carefully
You'll hear them play so merrily
They play their song
The whole day long
Spring, spring, spring

Rainbows
by Kaitlin Anderson

After a heavy rainfall
I look across the sky.
What I see with no surprise.
A simple rainbow.
Simple and pretty
Giving life to the sky.
See its radiant colors
Dash and dance across the sky.
As I walk it follows me
As I try to find the pot of gold.
Our fun must come to a end
Because it's getting dark outside.
One day I'll see you again.

Bird
by Ashton Pardun

Bird, bird in the sky
Flying above the midnight sky
Bird, bird in the sky
Flying as fast as the human eye

Colors
by Jasmin Garcia

White is the twinkle of a newborn star
Blue is the deepest, darkest ocean
Black is being taken afar
Turquoise is the smallest, littlest motion
Red is the loving and caring heart of a soul
Lime green is the newest grass in the springtime
Brown is a horse and her foal
Gold is the golden juice squirting from a lime
Many colors make other colors, but some people take them for granted

The Majestic Lion
by Ramya Balasingam

The proud lion throws back his shaggy head
And roars so loudly, frightening all.
Nothing fills anyone with such dread
As the sound of a lion's brawl.
He lets out a large bay
And shakes his mane as he is about to depart
To stalk his fearful prey,
And make them distraught.
He peers from behind a sandy boulder
Near a deer drinking water.
He waits silently and does not stir
As he is about to slaughter.
He lets out a roar, so loud, frightening the deer,
While others nearby tremble in fear.

I Am an American
by Devon Waegell

I am of America
It is water, ground, and sky
I am of its army
Fighting for what's right
I am of its flag
The colors Red, White, and Blue
I am of its history
From the beginning to its end
I am of its culture
Like yours, mine, and theirs
I am of its mountains
Sly, tall, and sturdy
I am of its rivers
Swift, smooth, and fast
I am of its people
Whatever color, shape, or size
I am an American
Strong, proud, and true

The Beast
by Austin Rice

It never laughs nor never cries.
It never sleeps nor never dies.
All it does from dusk till dawn,
Is make the soldiers die.

Dark Days
by Wyatt Parker

Dark days,
Light nights,
Nothing comes past my windows
Dark days
I lay in my bed all alone
Nothing but me
Dark days
Now it's night
I'm alright
No more dark days
Just light nights

The Lullaby
by Sally Chesnut

Your head on your pillow, your thoughts on your bed
Your worries and doubts, oh, what lay ahead?
The dreams and hopes that you wish to find
Circle around your anxious mind
The future, the past, you no longer know
What happened last summer or first winter's snow
Plenty caught up in your fears–it's true
A single note out of the blue
A song so sweet to melt each heart
To sing you goodnight, and sleep you start
Under the covers, warm and snug
A nighttime kiss and evening hug
The tune–a lullaby, quiet but strong
You lose your worries, gone with the song
You fall into a paradise, the land of snores and snooze
You think of other ways to win, instead of ones to lose
The song has given you courage, the courage to make things right
All in just a lullaby, the melody she sings goodnight

Pride In America
by Scene Wan

America, America
Where there's lots of good fellas.
People try,
They sometimes cry.
But in the end
They make the bend.
In America
Everybody feels so well-a.
People have pet dogs
And they both eat hot dogs.
America's hamburgers
They make you hunger.
Some people die
But it makes us survive.
We people live
So we can give.

Pride In America
by Janelle Le

America is the place to be.
America is a great country.
America is the best.
Even out in the west.
You can say whatever you want.
You can do whatever you want to do.
It's all up to you.
And what you want to do.
America is full of freedom.
But Barack Obama leads 'em.
He's the first black president.
And of course, it was meant.
Red, White, and Blue is the color of our flag.
And one of America's favorite games is tag.
You probably heard of it before.
So come join and so we can play some more!

Pride In America
by Connor Hankey

America is the place for me
Land of the brave, home of the free
Some people take this country for granted
I think America is the best on this planet
Our Founding Fathers wrote the "Declaration"
To make sure America was one great nation
In America there is freedom for all
For this freedom soldiers would fall
One thing that makes America a great place
We accept people from every race
All people in this nation have freedom of speech
In other countries this is out of reach
I am proud to wave the red, white, and blue
To these colors I will always stay true
In America I am free
I can be anything I want to be!

Amigos!
by Mariah Saldana

I love my friends
We'll stay together even when we're in Depends
My friends are great
I know you're jealous, but don't hate
My friends are spectacular
We have our own vernacular
My friends and I are crazy
Sometimes we think we're Jay-Z
My friends and I may be obnoxious,
But we're not noxious
We have a lot of inside jokes
Those sometimes cause laughter strokes
My friends and I are a little rowdy,
But we always make the sky seem less cloudy
You might think we're insane, or crazy, or whatever, but just so you know,
I love my friends

America
by Justin Shatz

Oh, how much I love America
And my love reaches Africa
To right here at Sutter
All the way to the Haiti disaster
From the white Hawaiian beaches
And to the Chinese peaches
With all the great food
We will never be rude
Here in America with the nicest people
With the sweet golden apples
With the little girls playing with their dolls
With the little boys playing with their kick balls
With our beautiful sky
And our fat flies
The beautiful bright sun
And we will have so much fun

Nature Is Forever
by Darrell Hampton

Nature is forever.
Nature might quiver,
If you are a river,
Or a big beaver.
Nature might shake,
If you are a mighty snake.
It might be still,
If you are a porcupine quill.
Nature might sing
If you're a lost ring.
The forest might shine,
If you are a big yellow light,
And if it is at midnight.
Nature is forever.

Oh How Beautiful
by Casandra Rose

Oh how beautiful
You are to me
You are graceful
And playful, so sweet
Oh how pretty
You are to me
Your mind made of smarts
And likeness at heart
Oh how cute
You are to me
Pride made like a tower,
Growing inches every hour
Oh how wonderful
You are to me
Your big brown eyes
Looking up at me
Oh my darling
You are very sweet
Oh how beautiful
You are to me

Angels
by Tori Taylor

Their smiles sweet
Their eyes innocent
With wings as white as snow.
That's how you know they're there.
But you shouldn't worry
They're here to help you.
"You must repent, and we'll forgive."
They smile, and reach out their hands.
You look at them sadly, not sure what to do
But you find yourself reaching, too
Taking their hands in yours.
Then you smile
You sprout your wings, and fly above
Then you sing in harmony with your angels.
Now you're with people who love you
So to yourself be true.

Dogs vs. Cats
by Avery Hillis

Dogs will be dogs
As they run free
They run in the forest
With massive amounts of glee
Cats are weird
As they walk over a bridge
They don't know how
To be filled with glee
Dogs on the other hand
Are as cool as an ice cream
On a hot day at the lake
They run like a chain saw
Mulching a tree that's covered
In a sticky sap that the bees love
Cats are slow as they walk
Cats are stupid, they always fall
Dogs are fast and very smart
They never fall as they cannot climb

The Forest
by Zara Phonhthydeth

As I walk through the forest
Seeing the plants
Big or small
All covered with ants
The mist on my skin
Heat all around
As I twirl
Avoiding a tree mound
Boom, pow
The thunder clashes
The rain pours
With wild lashes
The colors of the forest
The sounds of the forest
The nature of the forest
The forest itself

Colors
by Drew Roberts

Red is the blazing campfire.
Yellow is like the blooming flowers that I desire.
Green is the grass that grows without care.
Blue is the deep, deep ocean that many fish share.
How would you describe the colors?

The Fire
by Andrew Wilson

A fire hungrily licking at papers
The fire crackles like an evil man laughing.
The waves of heat against my skin.
The smoke rises from the ashes
Like a ghost rising from its earthly grave

America
by Leslie Parada

America the beautiful, America the great,
There are many beautiful things in all of its States,
Our president is Barack Obama,
He is America's first black president,
And Tiger Wood's scandals brought the drama,
The recession has made a dent,
In everybody's wallet, but people are still buying,
All the new clothes and all the new shoes,
And hey look what's on the news!
It's almost time for Arnold Schwarzenegger to step out of office,
Earthquakes are now occurring more often,
There was one in Baja California on Sunday, its magnitude was 7.2,
The earthquake wasn't as dangerous as it sounds,
But it still left people with frowns on their faces,
All in all, America is full of great places,
Full of beautiful sights and wonderful faces

Buddy
by Kimberlin Crist

Blond, shaggy hair, such a mess,
But I love it so much, none the less
Warm brown eyes, bright and shiny
It doesn't even matter that you're tiny
You bark at nothing, it drives me up the wall
Sometimes I think you won't stop at all
You play so rough,
Yet it just makes you tough
Sometimes at night you howl so long,
But I like to call it my good night song
You don't chase your tail
And you don't attack the man that delivers the mail
You can't roll over, can barely sit still
And you always try to climb up the windowsill
When you take a bath, you always get me wet,
But you most likely don't know better, I bet
You're my tiny friend, keeper of my secrets
I loved you from the moment we met
People call you dumb, a stupid mutt,
But you're my dog, my little Buddy

I Wonder
by Sierra Pell

Life is short,
Why must we waste it?
Our time is short,
But long like a novel.
Why are we here?
Was there a reason?
I am young,
But still I wonder.
"You are wise for your age,"
My mother compliments.
I wonder why we pollute
And kill this Earth.
Were we put here
To hurt and kill
Or ... make peace and do good?
I wonder why,
I wonder why.

Pride In America
by Steven Tanaka

America is our country
We live here
It is a beautiful place
It is our home
We must take care of our country
We must treat it with respect
It is a fun place
You can do almost anything in America
America is our country
It is the home to millions and millions of people
As a citizen it is our job to make America a better place
We must keep it safe and also clean
America is our country
We should be proud of America
It is the best
We must show our pride to the whole world
We should show how much we love our country
America

Goldie
by Gage Dixon

Love that dog
Like a mother loves her child
I said I love that dog
Like a mother loves her child
Love to play with her in the afternoons
Love to tell her, "Good girl"
And, "Great job"
She walks like a proud deer
Is strong like an athlete
I said she walks like a proud deer
And is strong like an athlete
She always was so hyper
And I thought she would live forever
I said she always was so hyper
And I thought she would live forever
I had her for a while
And I will see her again
I said I had her for a while
And I will see her again
I thought she would live forever

Crescent Moons
by Alexander Young

Crescent moons are always beautiful
My mom has a crescent moon necklace
Our cat has a crescent moon birthmark
Our table is the shape of a crescent moon
New moons become beautiful crescent moons
Moons are beautiful, whatever the moon,
But my favorite moons are crescent moons

Viva La America
by Mignot Berhanie

Oh, how I'm proud to be an American
Smelling freedom everywhere
It makes you want to stare at the beautiful sites
That you just can't compare
Oh, so what, Paris has the Eiffel Tower
America has something way better,
A great opportunity for my future
What more does America have to offer?
Like having great pride and honor
I love the freedom of speech
And how my schools teach
I love how there are so many different people
From being crazy, to being casual
From being funny, to being moody
Or from being you, to being me
I love my equal rights
And how we have civilized word fights
I love the culture here
Never get tired of it each year
I love how America has everything
I would be so betting
That you wouldn't find something
That isn't already here
I love that America is a country
With equal rights for everybody
I see many things on TV
One is that some people are just not lucky
To have the chance to live in an awesome country like me

A Kite Just As Love
by Sami Baker

A kite is a wondrous thing as it glides through the clear blue sky
And it soars through the blue crisp air just as love.
Love is a beautiful thing when it drifts through people's hearts
While it brings happiness to make an endless knot of great affection.

Kelp
by Marissa DeVogelaere

Reaching up for light
Swaying in the water's breeze
Surrounded with life

Pride In America
by Monica Lee

Each blade of grass
And every inch of road
Everywhere you hear a bass
And everything you sewed
The home in which you live in
Whether on mountain or ocean
Where you see many kin
And where's there lots of commotion
Each Olympic game you see
Has an American gold medalist
And every broken knee
Has a twisted wrist
Every election you vote in
Every NASCAR race you watch
Somebody has to win
But sometimes there is a rematch
Our world has no boundaries
Because everybody has freedom
Which includes many foundries
If everybody had wisdom

Pride In America
by Maya Campos-Young

America is filled with pride
It's where great ideas and people collide
We as a country are working together
To help children strive
To be alive
As children become adults
They become inspiring people
Who work everyday
To earn their pay
This country is incredible
Its knowledge spreads worldwide
It gives me great feelings inside
To know that I am in a place where it's happy
America is where I live
A place where people give
I shout its name
Oh America, no place is the same.

Pride In America
by Corey Louie

The land of the free,
Love in this country is key,
Beautiful places we all love to see,
Makes us feel happy and filled with glee,
Freedom of speech and rights like those,
Barack Obama is the president we chose,
Washington, D.C., is the center of it all,
We chose Obama in the fall,
We have fifty states,
From New York to the Golden Gate,
We respect our country, family, and friends,
In America there is always new trends,
We have the greatest places,
And the most wonderful faces,
But the best thing ever,
Is having friends forever.

My American Pride
by Greyson Horst

I am proud to be an American,
In the land full of freedom,
Where it is great to be human,
And I will proudly sing the anthem.
America provides great opportunities,
No matter who you are, whatever you want to be,
There are great colleges and universities,
You can be you and I can be me.
America is also beautiful within,
From cities with towers of buildings,
To nature with towers of mountain,
And the beach where children imagine their wings.
America's entertainment is the best,
With new technology for movies, and the games you try to win,
And an abundance of sports where the athletes need rest,
Once again, I love being an American.

Great America
by Alexis Hankins

Sweet land of liberty,
There is justice for all
Together we stand,
Apart we fall
We are hand in hand,
United as one
In this great land
That has just begun
The great waves
That lay below the rising sun,
And the shining gem encrusted caves
Some of the most beautiful parts
The home belongs to the brave
It's beauty captures other's hearts
Because America's beauty
Shows people where love starts

Pride In America
by Anthony Fukuhara

Take pride in America, the greatest place to be.
There are many sites to see.
People made these sites with pride.
It can make people cry.
See all of the amazing sites.
Some sites built by man took many days and nights.
Sights you can see are the five Great Lakes in Michigan.
If you liked what you saw, see it again.
People love admiring works of art.
The people who made these works of art were really smart.
A great work of art was the Grand Canyon.
It would be nice going there with a companion.
There were some sights that were greatly appreciated.
Then they became depreciated.
Come to America to see the great sites.
Some of these sites look really great at night.

Love America
by Anissa Maldonado

God bless America, land of the free,
Because this is where I want to be.
America, the beautiful, is the greatest of all,
Given to us by the courageous men and women
Who fought and fell and did it all.
We're lucky for our ability to say (speech) and
Believe (religion) what we desire,
Without being afraid of being killed or set on fire.
We vote for who we want because it's
An American privilege and right,
So we must keep going to the polls
To always keep this right of choice in sight.
We live in a land full of opportunity that has no bounds,
So never forget that with "hard work," it all will come around.
No matter who we are and where we are living,
Love America, because we're always so very giving.

Pride In America
by Selena Baker

America the great
Let freedom ring forever
It always has the top rate
We will say no never.
This country has its ups and downs
We have never given up
Fighting and pushing the bounds
Setting new limits is what we have done.
There have been new achievements all around
With NASA and the government changing
New discoveries are about
Our limits will not be ranging.
The United States of America is great
Our nation will have no end
Nothing can underestimate
Our nation and our pride in the USA.

My America
by Aengus Nelson

America is the home of my birth
The home of apple pie, hot dogs
The home of baseball
The best sport on earth
With Rhode Island so small
The Grand Canyon so big
Death Valley so low
The Rockies so tall
Hopper's "Night Hawks" at the diner
Jack Kerouac's "On the Road" a classic
Yo-Yo Ma on his cello
Bob Dylan's music, nothing finer.
Golden Gate Bridge over the sea
The Sears Tower in the clouds
Statue of Liberty so proud
This is what America means to me

School
by Josh Jamison

School is a great place to learn
Crammed with info on all subjects
Homework isn't that great though
Oh, why do we have so much homework?
On weekends too?
Like school or not, it's good for you

Economy
by Katrina Morin

The things that have happened in our economy today;

Everyone has to give up those little things of life
Cash is lost from those who need it a lot
Our loved ones are lost in debt
No one wins in this mess that others made for us to hold
Our houses are taken away from you and me
Money is everywhere else but our pockets
You are in debt for losing everything you love

Our economy is hurting all who are born and unborn.
Our economy.

Prejudice
by Emily Bassett

Running, running against a pale moon,
Does not know which road to take,
Cannot run, cannot hide,
What shadows all this running make,
The men with power did curse her dreams,
The men with power haunt her still,
And all of this, just one thing does mean,
Their own greedy cups they mean to fill,
And as the shining sun does come,
And as it will set again,
Off and on and will never be done,
Cursed by all these powerful men.

The Change
by Makenzie Evans

The dripping of ice everywhere
The snow melting away slowly
The cool wind rushing by like a runner
The otters swimming in the cold water
The trees slowly growing leaves back
The waterfall slowly falling apart
Flowers suddenly coming to life
Plants everywhere waving hello after a long winter
The sun's rays finally beat down
The change from winter to spring

Dogs
by Darcey Filsinger

Cute as a button
Small and innocent as a child
Well trained as an adult
Love in its eyes
A brand new collar
With a new tag
Shiny and in gold
And its name engraved
Bringing them home
To a new little bed
New water and food bowl
With a few toys
From a wet nose
To a little wet kiss
Showing its affection
And waiting for a ball to be thrown
Memories in a book
From when it first came home
When it first gnawed a bone
To a first training session
Hopping up on the couch
Getting told to get down
A sad look on its face
And you forgave them
Coming home from the doctors
With a sad look on your face
Packing up collars, toys, bowls and its bed
Pulling out the book of memories
And sitting there crying ...

3rd Place

Ariel Riley

Ariel is very active at school
where she is President of Student Council.
She likes to keep abreast of the latest fashion trends,
but couples that with her own unique style.
In her spare time, Ariel says she likes to read
and watch some of the more creative videos on YouTube.

Each Other
by Ariel Riley

"Mommy," she says in a scared voice
"Where is our home going?"
"Sicily," the mother says to her child in her loving voice
"We shall find a new home. Nothing to worry 'bout now"
"Well, how's Cassidy?" she panics
"She is in my arms and well," the mother responds
She turns to the bars that are as cold as ice
Dazed by the sight of flames thousands of feet above and in our home
"But what do we have left, Mommy?"
"Each other," she whispers

2nd Place

Will Griffin

This young author is an exceptional student athlete
who enjoys competing in a number of sports
including football, baseball, basketball, and tennis.
Will can often be found hanging out with his friends,
but still makes plenty of time to spend
with his little five-year-old brother, Luke.

The Last Time
by Will Griffin

There had to be a last time
I went out to play on my old swing set
In the backyard, at the bottom of a hill
There had to be a last time
I waved to my dad through the window
As he was going to work
There had to be a last time
I played Hide-and-Seek with my little sister,
Or a last time I climbed our Japanese maple tree,
Or rode down our driveway on my blue bike with training wheels
There had to be a last time
My mom bandaged my wounded knees
There had to be a last time
I saw my granddad before he saw Jesus
I have done so many things for the very last time

1st Place

Amber Rose Granger

It's no surprise that this talented young lady
lists writing poetry and short stories
as one of her favorite hobbies.
Amber says she also has a special interest
in European and Asian cultures.
In fact, when she's not spending time with her sister or friends,
she's aspiring to learn a number of new languages,
including Japanese, Polish, and Russian.

I Will Rip Their Wings
by Amber Rose Granger

Butterflies fluttered past me,
Their water-colored wings flowing with the wind,
I wanted to reach out and tear each one of their wings apart.
They had taken Mommy away.
Daddy had told me that the butterflies took Mommy to Heaven.
I wanted my revenge today,
I wanted them to bring Mommy home.
Daddy told me to only wish they could.
Each butterfly I see, I will rip their wings and burn them,
I will rip and burn until they bring Mommy back.

Division III

Grades
8-9

Wind Rage
by Kevin Axelrod

The wind rushes past with force and meaning
And so the trees nearby are leaning
With one more breath, they could fall down
And cause commotion in the town
No fog dares to settle in the bay
As it will be at risk of being swept away
The wind whistles and squeals with a voice eerie
Showing signs of resentment and fury
It sprints up the mountains, and without instruction
Tears down trees and causes destruction
Although wind has tempers, I can't resist temptation
To go out and feel that great windy sensation
It's in quite a hurry, so it won't stay forever
But when it is, it will make quite an endeavor

The Turnaround
by Micah Mitchell

Sometimes we get down
And we're all turned around
We don't know what to do
And we're even feeling blue
But for this terrible feeling
I know something that's healing
Free's not expensive
And it's comprehensive
You just close your eyes and say,
"Lord, I need you more today"
And before you know
You'll be good to go
Though the feeling is divine
Beware–there will come a time
When the devil will fight back
Be ready for his attack

Unclear Mind
by Kyndrierra Tatum

Unstable with an attitude
What does that tell you?
There are always questions unanswered and stories untold
So much confusion to fog my mind
Trying to change will never be simple
How do I get this straight?
Always considering the "what ifs"
The dos and don'ts of the world
Should I have done this or should I have done that, can't figure it out
Dealing with love, infidelity, relations, and multiple crises
So much affection for such a person, how much longer do I hold it in?
Only one person to talk to, to share true fondness with
There when I need her, but unable to solve every solution
Appreciative when I need to be, but sometimes doesn't get me far
How does kind answer questions in my head,, the hurt in my heart
Can people know what they do or feel the pain they cause?
Until a brighter day I'll be looking for my conclusion
And until then, I stay in my unclear mind

The True Colors of a Fellow
by Destiny Wesson

Dark? Light? Tan? Yellow?
What are the true colors of a fellow?
He wants to be your buddy,
Wants to be your friend.
He cries when you don't accept him,
And hates it when you don't let him in.
After she thinks about it, rewinds, and presses play,
She skips back to reality and finally must say;
"Hey, good lookin', you wanna go on a date?"
At first he was blue from sadness,
Now he turns orange, that represents warmth and gladness!
He gets red hot when the girl's thoughts turn into a reality.
They go on a date.
Don't get home too late.
He goes in for a kiss,
Doesn't miss!
He goes from blue to orange and from red to yellow.
These are all true colors of a fellow.

Friends
by Sharnell Fuller

Friends are forever
Friends do crimes together
Friends stick together, though they might fight
But I have a friend and we are so tight
Fussing and fighting like Tom and Jerry,
We stay together and still remain cheery

Sweet Dreams
by Angelina Delgado

I drift asleep
While I'm sleeping I count sheep
And unconsciously wonder where they may go
So I sit back and enjoy their show
I sleep peacefully, dreaming sweet dreams
And then the sheep cross three streams
Then they cross a mountaintop
I sit there hoping they won't drop
And now I lie awake
Thinking of how life can take

A Snowflake Tragedy
by Skyler Ronna

Snowflakes flurry as I gaze at the stars.
These snowflakes' journey has been far,
Yet most won't survive past the first step.
Too cold to ascend to where water's kept.
As the snow falls to Earth, do not be fooled:
Not enough accumulation to keep it all cool,
And ever more snow with each step is slain.
The weather warms up; the snow melts to rain.
What a rare occurrence; we'll never know
In a singular snowflake, a piece of snow.

Dreaming of Sunshine
by Miranda Gerhardt

As I lay around in my cozy bed
The one thing that I dread
Is the coldness that lies ahead
As my albino skin weeps
The only thing, for me to do, is sleep.
I dream of the bright sunshine
And sweet summertime.
Flowers, sun, thoughtless minds,
Just can't wait for summertime.
Running with the wind, howling at the people,
Never thinking,
Never blinking
Won't let a moment pass me by
Oh, how I dream of sweet summertime.
The grass so green, beaches so playful,
Now this is a time where all should be peaceful.
The time for sun is coming near,
But it's taking its precious,
Oh, how I dream of sweet sunshine

Winter Mornings
by Colin Paisley

Waking up
Going downstairs
You look outside
Snow falling to the ground
Falling all around
Doesn't even make a sound
Going back upstairs
Able to fall back to sleep
Not needing to go to school
Zzzzz ...

Classmate, O' Classmate
by Sara Banter

Why are you so caught up
In the evil of all popular?
You've got it all poured into a cup.
Treating people so mean,
Is a cruel sight that I have seen.
I know on the inside that you are so sweet.
Please show it –know it– and hold it to keep.

Conflicting Emotions
by Samantha Spell

Every day is different
And with it comes a new emotion
Some days sad, some happy
But never the same
No day ever comes back
As with people
Everyone is equal, but never alike
Emotions have an astonishing impact
But never the same feel
With all the emotions we come by
We improve with every day

Crush
by Cheyanne Alameda

You come around every day
And when you do
I feel butterflies
I do not know what I would do
If anything happened to you
You're like my brother
Yes, you are
And you'd fight for me
If anyone tried to cause me harm,
But I know what I have to say,
You're my crush
So please don't go away

The Storm
by Libby Long

The storm was coming
We saw the lightning
We all screamed
We saw a shadow
The door opened
We screamed
But it was my parents

Lamps
by Bailey Smith

You can be short and you can be tall
You can be fat and you can be skinny
You can be pretty or you can be bare
You are always by my bedside
I use you when darkness starts to rule
Your talent helps me improve my skill
Your talent sometimes gets old and in need to be changed
Your use is needed for lots of things,
But sometimes people give you another talent that you must obey
"Snap!" and you're on, "Clap!" and you're on
Just a command and you're on
So don't feel bad if you feel unwanted
Because people need you in the darkest of times
We love your presence and you love ours
You let us know by shining brighter

My School Day
by Tyler Esposito

I sit in class all day
For seven hours where I stay
There are six classes for a day
Except students talk and play
This is a Catholic school
Where every person is kind and cool
Kindergarten to eighth grade is what we teach
And preschool is where they learn how to be neat
That's my story of my day
Now I really want to stay

Fear Is Not a Solution
by Kacie Crawford

There is a loud bang at the door.
I lie in my bed and listen to the screaming on the other side.
"Go away! Please leave me alone!"
The banging on the door is silenced;
The door begins to rattle, the knob falls off.
I crawl out the window and run.
I hear him hollering and cussing at me,
But I'm not looking back
I just keep running as the car roars like an angry cougar.
I hide in the brush as he drives past me
I make a run for it, back to the house,
I gather all my things that are needed,
Grabbed the phone and called the police.
Headlights shine outside the window, the car shuts off.
He's fussing and stomping everywhere for me;
I quietly go out the window
And hide underneath the house with my things.
The cops have made it; I carefully crawl out
And watch as they finally take him away.

Great-Grandpa
by Mackenna Gott

When he died
I cried
I sit at his grave
And forgave
God for taking him away
But I knew he was through the gateway
Of Heaven and with my great-grandma
Him, happier than ever
Watching over me and the beloved
I sit and pray
For one day
I hope to see him
On my everlasting journey
I sit at his grave
And forgave
When he died
I cried

Oceans
by June Janke

I look out at the ocean
It looks so calm, like everything is at peace
I know everything is in its place
Everything simply does its job not realizing the impact it has on the ecosystem
I close my eye and try to picture how it would feel, to be in my place,
Not having to question if I belong
I open my eye and see the sun making the water shimmer
I wonder if I do have a place, if I have meaning in this world
I decided to clear my mind of the worries and bad thoughts
I try to focus on the pure beauty of the ocean

Christmas Morning
by Daniel Jessen

Christmas morning comes every year always
We put up a big decorated tree
Along with nativity manger scenes,
Snowmen, Santa Clauses, and the reindeer
Then we head out to find the perfect gift
Looking for the best bargains to be found
Now we are ready for Christmas morning

Forever
by Brittany Johnson

Marriage means not letting go if never,
It means holding on at least forever.
Marriage is a place where couples fight,
But it's that same person who will hold you day and night.
Marriage is a time when things can get rough,
But the bond between the two is more than enough.
Marriage is a circle that never ends,
It's about two lovers who are also best friends.
Marriage is a box that you put your trust in,
But it's also like a carnival game, it can be very hard to win.
Marriage says, "Until death do us part."
Marriage is someone who gave you their soul and heart.

Heart Strings
by Tori Stone

Take time to treat tenderly our hearts.
Emotions escape our mind's eye; our soul they do not depart.
A lullaby sounds lightly on a little one's ear
As precious peace springs forth in a tear.

Lives As Seasons
by Sharlet Johnson

Live, love, and laugh: three words that everyone experiences
Taken away by an ugly word, depression
You only have this one life to live to the fullest
Take control of it, before it passes like seasons

Friday Night Game
by Brian Filer

The waiting is over
And game day is here
As we go through the day
The game draws near
The Friday game lights
Are finally on
We've been waiting
All day long
Here comes the kickoff
The ball is in the air
Our return men run
As fast as they dare

You
by Denise Roof

Talking to you tonight,
Telling you I want to be held tight,
Telling you I need you in my life,
To keep me away from the knife,
Telling you I love you in every possible way,
Hearing everything you have to say.

If Tomorrow Starts Without Me
by Catherine Deaton

If tomorrow starts without me
I want you to know
I loved you dearly
And didn't want to go
I know how much you love me
As much as I love you
I wish this didn't happen
But it did, this nightmare is true
The last minute I pulled the trigger
The thought crossed through my head
A life without you
Was a scary life ahead
I changed my mind the last minute
And here I am in hell
I didn't want to be here
I'd rather be in jail
At least I would be with you
And see your face every day
I never wanted you
To ever go away
If tomorrow starts without me
And we are far apart
Just think about the love
We shared deep in our hearts

Keep Moving Forward
by Tori Hansen

Keep moving forward even when the snow falls
Cold, shining crystals covering the ground
Overtime, it begins to gather
Everything seems perfect as the cold, shining crystals fall from the sky
Suddenly it stops, everything stops
The snow disappears, never to return
Tears stream down your face
Your heart begins to ache
But you must keep moving forward with the rest of the world

Caged Bird
by Jennifer Teague

Closed in, cold, alone
I wish to travel in the open sky
But no, for I am stuck here on the ground
A bird trapped in a cage
While the flock flies ahead, I am alone
Forever to be forgotten
A mystery left unsolved
A life that hasn't fulfilled
A dream that never came true
For I am a bird trapped in a cage
While you fly, I watch
While you soar, I wait
For the one person to let me free
But for now
I am a bird trapped in a cage

Why Try If We Can't Win?
by Joshua Conard

Why try if we can't win–
Drink a soda
To wash down the Vicodin
Then I start to spin
And want to make din-din
But I can't cook
Because I'm a crook.
My food I took,
So now take a look
As we cry,
Tears rolling from each eye.
I gave life a try
Vicodin's kickin' in
While I say, "Bye"
I overdose and die.

Letting Go
by Elizabeth Keesee

Letting go is the hardest part
Emptiness and main for the broken heart
What is easy for him, the letting go
Is hardest for her, her heart says no
In her thoughts and in her dreams
In love alone or so it seems
She cries awake in her sleep
The pain is hidden, it cuts so deep
A smile and laugh throughout the day
Costs so much she cannot pay
Becoming what she feared to be
A shell of a person, please help me
I have lost my love, my heart, my friend
A mistake I hope to never make again

Eyes Speak Miles (DV)
by Rachel Hynds

There you are
With a cloud over you
You're a star
No matter what you do
I know we've just met
But I'm falling fast
And you may not like me yet
But this crush will last
She's trying to steal you away
I thought she was my friend
Betrayal 101- with a hint of dismay
This would be my end
I wish I could see your eyes
The door to your soul
Are they full of lies?
Or are you pure gold?
You comfort my soul
And put sunshine in my eyes
You make me whole
These baby blues speak miles

Winter
by Aditya Srinivasan

The bitter cold bites my skin,
It shreds the remaining warmth in my soul,
Winter stabs the Earth with a pin,
It makes this world as bleak as coal.
I look around to see what survives,
And then to my disgust,
I see dead trees and empty hives,
The world has turned so unjust.
As I lean against the great big oak,
I feel a heartbeat come to a halt.
I pray that any person, any bloke,
Brings me happiness in a vault.
And as the bitter cold bites my skin,
I lose hope for any light.
And after finding none of my kin,
I conclude, "Winter, winter wins the fight."

Seasons
by Mihir Altekar

Spring
Cordial cool spring breeze
World wakes up after winter
The cycle begins
Summer
Earth at its fullest
The heat brings much warmth and joy
The cycle prospers
Fall
Summer is over
Rich chromas seen in the leaves
The cycle diminishes
Winter
Sight of pristine snow
It covers Mother Nature
The cycle is done

Pox the Hamster
by Claudia Li

The best gift I got from a friend long ago,
Was something alive with bright eyes and a nose.
His mother and father had many a kid,
But Pox was the hamster with my highest bid.
I gave him–my new friend–a nice place to live,
And he was the best gift a best friend could give.

Colors Constantly Changing
by Grace Woo

People say they're dying
Because their leaves are flying
People enjoy the trees' last flush
Of color before the great hush
But one stands still
On top of the hill,
Apart from all the rest,
Posing, like she is the best
Like humans who lose their hair,
The other trees stand so bare
Standing there with a luscious green,
That one tree creates a beautiful scene
Colder and colder the climate can be
Greener and greener becomes the tree
Soon enough, snow silently descends,
And the season of red finally ends

Life
by Kavassha Smith

Life is short, life comes with pain
We live and we learn life lessons
We lose people, we gain people
The ones who love you will stay
The ones who don't, slowly drift away
These lessons we learn in life truly come with a meaning and reason
Life is a take-or-keep situation
We all live, learn, love, and have to go someday
Live your life good while you have it.
Life is too short to waste!

A Dream
by Wiley Cofield

I dream of being a star with fame
I dream of fans calling my name
I have always wanted to be that guy
Want to see my name in lights in the sky
I would be the most popular man alive
More so than a queen bee in a hive
I will make people know who I am
When they hear me they'll know it's not a scam
I will do it, make my dream come true
You can do it, try it too
I am going to show everybody
That I can do it, be a somebody

Love
by Lillian Divine

You ask me what I value, the answer is you
You ask me if I care, and I say I do
You ask me if I'll leave, I say never
You ask me if I love you, I say forever

Cougars vs. Bears
by Daysha Caldwell

It's a football game!
There's no time to be lame.
Let's fight,
Through the night!
The Cougars are here
Let's have some cheer!
We are playing the Bears,
But nobody cares!
We are here to win
So let's cheer again
The Bears think they're strong,
But they are so wrong.
The Cougars won the game!
We have no shame.
Thanks to every fan
We are going to Disney Land!

Little Dark-Skinned Girl
by Kelia Smith

Little dark-skinned girl,
Do you know the story your skin tells,
The culture that is held within?
Be proud little dark-skinned girl, because your skin like night is beautiful
Your rich soulful voice is beautiful
All your dips and curves are beautiful
Little dark-skinned girl don't be ashamed of your complexion
Follow your own direction and dare to be different
Little dark-skinned girl you've got power in every step
Because of the story your skin tells
Little dark-skinned girl, love your skin

To Live and Die In the Streets
by Devonte Collins

My hustle is a deadly game
I should be in the street hall of fame
You grow up with people, just to see them fall dead
When they're in their casket, it's like they're in bed
When they put them in the ground, it's the final farewell
The streets can be Heaven or Hell
Everywhere I go it's blood on a knife
In this world you only get one life
In the streets it's Crips, Bloods, and G's
Kids in these streets don't even know their ABC's
One day this will all come to an end
There will be no home, no family, no friends
My mother couldn't believe her ear
'Cause the one she loved dear
Is now dead and gone
I was shot and killed on my way home
Now it's my turn to be in the casket
Everyone brings flowers in a basket
The stuff I did can't be beat
This is the day I lived and died in the L-town streets

I Am
by Courtney Hanaway

I am a dancer with a dream
I wonder if I'll ever be the one chosen
I hear how hard it is to get in
I want to be the one
I am a dancer with a dream
I pretend I'm the only one out there on stage
I feel the lights beaming down upon me as sweat drips from my body
I touch my feet to the ground, turning, leaping, dancing
I worry that I won't make it out there in the dance world
I cry as my body aches from the day before, all the disciplined hard work
I am a dancer with a dream
I understand there's many dancers out there
I say, "I am the one"
I dream about being the best one out there
I try to be the one who stands out most
I hope to be the one
I am a dancer with a dream

Empty Space
by Venesha Sasser

The empty space that was once filled,
Where happiness once stood.
Only now seen as water
An empty body
Drained by love
Existence taken as though it were something so valuable
Only space
Dusty, empty.
Echoes, screaming, cries for something,
Something of existence
Something of soul, love, true happiness
Something eager, or of true meaning
Something that can fill this empty space
Something of color, charisma, true character.
Something that can only make that empty space visible.
Something with which I can fill the empty space and make it full again.

Forever Friendship
by Kailey Wright

June 3, 1912–you're both born.
You haven't met each other yet, but you will.
Samantha and Emily, your names that you haven't learned.
Years 1 to 10.
The start of a long, long life.
You'll learn to play, maybe with dolls or with a ball
You'll learn to eat with those funky utensils
You'll go to school,
Where you will learn about those things called letters and words.
You'll start to learn more, about each other, about the world.
You will meet new people,
But no one who could replace one another.
You will meet boys, think they have cooties
But then learn to like them.
You will finally learn those names that were given to you
When you were both born on that special day.
Years 10 to 30.
You are older now and will experience many new things.
You will learn about "loving" someone
You will learn about what the gross, scary, interesting, fun,
And happy moments are like
You will learn about people who changed the world,
And want to be one of them someday
You will learn about being patient, enduring, caring, and adventurous
You will finish your full education
You will learn what real love is
You will find that special someone
You'll get that magical "rock" that will sit on that special finger
You will start a family
Years 30 to 60.
You have a family now and your dream home
You'll learn how hard life can be
You will become a grandma
You'll experience things out in the world
You will travel all over the world
Maybe to Hawaii or to Australia
Years 90 to 100
The last years of your entire life
You will finally see that same place
That you were both born in
You'll realize just how important
Your family, friends, and life are
You'll feel the worst pain in the world:
The pain of losing your family and life,
But most importantly, your friend:
The one you grew up with
The one who will never let you go
The one who was there for you when you were hurt
The one who will forever always be in your heart
And the one who will always keep you in her heart
Samantha. Emily ... September 10, 2010.

Mouse
by Amber Rogers

Around the door
Without a sound
Across the floor
See it bound
In the fridge it goes
For some cheese,
But then it froze
Because someone sees
For he's out of time
He must hurry
Because of his crime
Here comes the cat, Mr. Furry
Through the living room
Here comes Mrs. Pound
Dodging the broom
Finally he's safe and sound

I Am
by Lexi Barney

I am independent and confused
I wonder if I will always be this way
I hear what I want to hear and block out the rest
I see a perfect world at peace
I want what I sometimes don't need
I am independent and confused
I pretend that my life is perfect
I feel the breeze through my hair
I touch the shingles of my roof
I worry that death is near
I cry when something is hurt
I am an independent and confused person
I understand life is not fair
I say I'm fine but I'm hiding the pain
I dream of what I want my life to be
I try to forget everything bad
I hope to let go of the past
I am independent and confused

The Mockingbird's Song
by Erin Wang

The mockingbird sits in her nest
She clicks her delicate beak, once, then twice
She tucks her smooth feathers beside her chest
And begins her beautiful song
Her clear voice rings among the trees
As she sings to awaken nature
The first to respond is a gentle breeze
Which she commands with her beautiful song
She sings of winter's death and the birth of spring
And the wind draws power from the lingering notes
She strengthens the wind until it is fiercely blowing
All the while she never stops her beautiful song
The wind blows away the last flakes of snow
The bird then proceeds to wake the flowers
She sings until the ground seems to glow
Flowers raise their heads, heavy with sleep, to listen to her beautiful song
She proceeds with her final act
Her music reaches a crescendo
And nature's full glory is about to come back
She is nearing the end of her beautiful song
Animals wake and leaves unfold
From the dull gray landscape
Colors explode
All is silent as the mockingbird ends her beautiful song

Young Man From France
by Tim Robinson

I knew a young man from France
He loved to sing and dance
He fell to the ground
Then twirled around
Then got back up to prance

War
by Trever Nielsen

Stop the war! Stop the war!
But still our boys are on a distant shore
Fighting in a rain which pours and pours,
Fighting a battle to rock their cores
They are given a rifle and led to a trench,
Which will soon be filled with bloody stench
Of friends and comrades they once knew
Who now encompass a giant tomb
It is a war started by the old and fought by the young
And the battle songs have all been sung
In the rain and bloodied shale
From Desert Storm to Passchendaele

I Am
by Alexis Wildman

I am self-conscious and shy
I wonder if I will ever grow out of it,
I hear that people do
I see people grow up and blossom
Like flowers, pretty and perfect
I want to be like them too
I am self-conscious and shy
I pretend to be something I'm not
I feel like I live a lie
I touch my face to make sure it's me
I worry that my true self will fade away
I cry about all the things I'm not
I am self-conscious and shy
I understand I'm supposed to stay true to myself
I say, "I will," each day
I dream of that day when it will actually happen
I try to make that day come sooner
I hope it is tomorrow, but for now
I am self-conscious and shy

Beauty Beyond the Black
by Courteney Coots

I know of an ugly, black, rain cloud, cold in all his ways;
To the average eye he has no source of interest or beauty,
But only seems to sadden
The dark and lifeless day.
To make known his anguish and sorrow
He bitterly spews out lightning,
Yet I see something quite magical about him
Even though he is so frightening.
For this somber rain cloud knows
He is looked upon in pity,
But the man who does not see his gift
Is the one who is not so witty.
For this gloomy, yet radiant cloud
When he begins to shed a tear,
Makes the delightful sound of abundant rain
So brilliant and so clear!

Us
by Amy Chraft

Like twins we may seem
But we have many differences in between,
For her brown hair matches her eyes
My blonde shines in the light,
Though she is a year older
I'm still tougher;
We stand stronger together
We haven't known each other for our whole lives
But our hearts love as though we have,
Sentences and phrases we laugh at all day
The Keeper holds them safe,
Even though the blood that runs through our veins
Is not the same;
There you'll always be
My Sissy
–Dedicated to Morgan K. Debisschop

When I'm Sad
by Taylor Myers

I see light blue
I feel like it's raining only on me
I feel like I'm dying over and over again
It's like I'm watching another life that isn't mine
I like to be in the darkness
I dream that I am not alive, that I am dead
I feel sad when I think about my past
And about all of the bad things that had happened to me
When I am in a corner all by myself, I feel happy
I feel better when I think about the things all by myself
I like it when I don't have to tell anyone what is going on in my life
I feel better when no one talks to me, when I am in the darkness
I like to be alone and in the pitch black
I put my head under the covers in the morning so that I will be in the darkness
I like to sit in a dark room and when no one doesn't turn on the light.

The Silver Atom
by Martravian White

The two symbols for silver are A and G.
The price of silver is too valuable for me.
Although it glistens and shines
It still can't be mine.
Although silver's atomic number is 47
It still makes you want to fall back into Heaven.
And speaking of this 47,
Silver density is so close to eleven.
It is highly valued and costs a lot
You'll probably have to sell your lot.
It is classified as a transitional metal
It is something you wouldn't want to put on your pedal.
Silver is used in quarters, nickels, dimes,
And can also be used in rhymes.
Silver neutron is 61
I know you wonder how it could be done.
I bet you didn't know silver's atomic mass is 107.

My True Love
by Samie Sass

My true love is the most beautiful man.
He is tall, funny, caring, smart, and handsome.
He is mine; he is not even close to tan.
If you take him I will hold you ransom.
He is more albino if you ask me.
But he is not that mighty though, I am.
He shines in the light if you can see,
Theoretically. Sitting at a dam,
At our creek. We had a castle down there too.
When we were little of course, it was fun.
Before we part I say, "Hun, I love you."
He calls me Sweetheart and I call him Hun.
All I can see when we kiss are white doves.
As you can see we're truly in love.

Hoof Prints
by Kylie Morrill

Hoof prints in the sand
By the sparkling ocean
Freedom is calling

Enjoy the Little Things
by Anthony Allio

When you wake, and the day begins,
The trees brush and the bird sings,
You're already awake but your alarm rings,
Gotta enjoy the little things.
When even the dullest thing gleams,
And on the cloudiest day, the sun beams,
When average people feel like kings,
Gotta enjoy the little things.
When a bird waves its battered wings,
With all the magic that summer brings,
When you'd rather have love than diamond rings.
Gotta enjoy the little things.

Music Is Me
by Michelle Page

The way you bring me up
When I am down
Your sound envelops me completely
The way you tell my story
When I'm afraid
Your meaning defines me
The way you live
Without really breathing
Your life ... is me
Music is my life
Music is my soul
Music is me

Don't Fear the Storm
by Logan Nicholas

Each day has its ups and downs
It makes you smile, it makes you frown
One moment the sun makes you warm
And just as suddenly it begins to storm,
But do not fear this up and down
The good times will come back around
So please take my advice to heart
Or that storm will tear you apart

Dreams
by Erin Collins

How can I dream
When I already have you?
You're faithful and true,
I needn't worry about you.
When was the last time
You looked at any girl but me?
That is a stupid question,
I am all he sees,
Just like to me
He is the only thing.
How can I dream
When my heart and mind
Are already filled
With the image of him?

Heartache
by Donna Cox

Why does he ignore me?
What have I done wrong?
Wasn't he the one that put the pain in my heart?
All I've done for him and what I would have done.
All I have sacrificed, my love, my heart, my soul, my mind.
What did I do to make him want to hurt me this way?
All I did was surround him with my love.
Was it my smile that threw him overboard?
Or was it my laugh? Maybe it was my looks,
The way I pucker my lips or pop my hips?
Whatever it was, it threw him overboard enough that he wanted to hurt me.
Whatever it was that made him want to hurt me, it worked 'cause I hurt so bad.
He pierced my heart with his harsh words.
Betting against his friend that he would make me give in.
Telling everyone that he was done with me 'cause I wouldn't.
Maybe that was the reason he wouldn't kiss or touch me, me not giving in.
Whatever the reason was, his words hurt me.
When I found out about them, it wasn't from him but others.
So why does he ignore me?
What have I done wrong?

The Drowning Sharks
by Owen Craver

Boyle scored against his own team last night, how sad
The Sharks choke again in the playoffs, how sad
Goodbye Marleau, Thornton, and Boyle
The Sharks put their fans through such toil!
Every year it's the same story;
Win all season, then lose, so gory
Every season they cannot find the way
They say next year will be different,
But we all know it will be the same
Maybe they don't realize
It's time for change in San Jose

Peace, Love, War, Hate
by Chance Farrar

Peace, love
War, hate.
Money, greed
Sorrow, grief.
Freedom, charity
Harmony, growth.
Peace, love
War, hate.

False Promises
by Charlotte Fernimen

What allows hope to exist in the midst of anger and destruction?
What allows dreams to flourish amongst the sorrows and despairs of this world?
Do hopes and dreams have a purpose,
Or are they merely fleeting glimpses of our longings and desires that will never be?
Something we wish was, but shall not come to pass?
All is nothing more than false promises that blow away like the sands of time.
Hopes, dreams, faith, and wishes are all connected by a fragile thread.
A thread made of what makes us human.
Of what makes us capable of love and compassion.
Everything within this thread is likewise connected.
This thread represents humanity, humanity represents each of us,
And so this cycle continues on and on,
Never truly ending but yet never truly being.
For can humanity really be so easily defined
If we are all so different in our dreams and wishes?
If the intertwinement of humanity is real,
Then we must all have connections to each other.
Connections that we cannot see, but yet are.
We are all connected by the false promises of what we whisper alone in the dark.
Connected by what we never speak of, but yet all know.
Inside we all know that what we hope, dream, and desire
Amounts to nothing in this world of pain and suffering.
It is this acknowledgment that leads to the discovery of the truth within ourselves.
The truth about fate and destiny.
For fate and destiny are all based on the idea
That we do not control our own actions for our own future
That is because we don't have any control over the false promise that we call life.

Freedom
by Emily Guzman

Left to cry in the solitude of nothing,
Held in the arms of long lost fates
I am alone, but I speak to everyone,
Confessing my forgotten sins
I am enveloped in hope,
The wind whispers forgiveness
The earth radiates faith
A deep breath brings freedom,
Entrusting myself with me,
The world is brighter,
Suddenly vibrant,
A road is uncovered–
I never look back.

If You Look
by Veronica Holloway

If you look in my eyes
You will see the sadness
If you look at my cheek
You will see the trail of my tears
If you look under my clothes
You will see the bruises
If you look at my heart
You will see it is broken
If you look in my head
You will get scared
If you look at my life
You will see the misery
If you listen to my soul
You will hear the screaming and fears
If you look at my goals
You will see they are far from near
If you stand back and look
You will see the pain of mine
But only if you look
With your heart and not your eyes

Cry Out
by Erika Kawaguchi

Watching, wishing, waiting, wanting.
Head pounding, heart racing.
Cry out, cry out! Please spare his life!
What's that? A noise?
A saving grace? No.
Watching, wishing, waiting, wanting.
Arms straining, muscles screaming.
Cry out, cry out! Please spare his life!
No, please don't! No.
Watching, wishing, waiting, wanting.
Limbs thrashing, lungs burning,
Cry out, cry out! Please one last time!
No, too late! Far too late.
It's done. It's over.
Cry out, cry out! What have they done?
Watching, wishing, waiting, wanting.
And as he falls, with his one last breath,
He breathes a smile, finally at rest.
Screaming, crying, fighting, angry.
Watching, wishing, waiting, wanting.

Moving On
by Bobby Ketscher

The easy days are gone
Now I am moving on
It is like a cold beach
I cannot see very far
The waves get in my way so I have to move
I feel like a lone crab in the middle of nothing
Just moving on
There is nobody around except the cold waves
That try to push me from my path
I try to move but I am just too slow
Moving on
It is cold and wet around me
As I am entombed beneath the earth
I cannot see my hands nor hear my voice
Just moving on

The Chase
by Heather Morgan

The dog's legs went rigid. She sniffed in the cool air.
She jumped down from my arms and just knew what was there.
She went scampering across the lawn to what awaited.
And there sat a kitten who did not look elated.
The dog went running and running, closer and closer to who's gone.
With the small kitten in the lead, the quick chase was finally on.

Termination
by Karen Mac

Hearts beating together–faster, faster
Cremating the world's remains with their lies
The knowing gods stare at the disaster
Picking and choosing who lives and who dies
Searching brutally for the purest souls
For a heart which endures with love and might
Finding finally two wonderful wholes
Which are pure and innocent as snow white
As precious life by lives taken away
And the buildings burn, now all left's rubble
In an abandoned place two people lay
Warm by each other, no thoughts of trouble
Lying softly in a soothing embrace
In the hopes that with them they'll bring on grace

Prisoner To My Emotions
by Heidi Garcia

Sad,
Alone,
Different,
They bind my hands in invisible handcuffs,
Pain,
Fear,
Misery,
Locks me in a lonely cell,
Anger,
Rage,
Insanity,
Isolates me in an inescapable prison ...
Of my emotions

Haiku
by Vimohana Popli

For simple haiku,
No need for a high IQ,
Count their syllables.

Ode To My Piano
by Alisha Morales

Oh, keys of black and white;
I slide my fingers across you,
To make music.
The notes dance across the page,
Sliding down,
Waiting for their songs to be told.
An expression, a story,
To tell something; a message to teach.
My feet reach the pedals,
And touch them ever so lightly.
You help me create music.
Sold many times,
Passed through many hands; generations.
You still play.
You've become cracked,
Your keys worn,
But you still create music.
Though your music now hushed,
And you are long forgotten,
Your music still remains.

Grandma's House
by Nikki Cadotte

(I see) The lonely clouds in the bluest sky above me
The glistening lake beneath my feet.
(I hear) The lovely, enchanting song of the bird, lost in the trees around me
The crashing waves bouncing against the rocks, spraying me with trickles of water.
(I smell) The sweet, succulent scent of honeysuckle calling out my name
The lush smell of pine trees surrounding me in every direction.
(I taste) The bittersweet taste of salt riding the breeze coming off the lake
The taste of a juicy, cherry lollipop on my tongue.
(I touch) The hard, rocky gravel between my fingers
The water, as cool and soothing as lemonade on a hot summer's day.
(I feel) The calming sense of peace.

Spring, My Darling, Spring
by Austin Powers

Spring, spring, my favorite child
All the others are reconciled
When spring blooms
And thunder shouts, "Boom!"
Spring brings rain
Like winter brings snow.
And summer brings heat
As we all know.
But nothing gold can stay
So ashes to ashes and dust to dust
When spring, my darling spring
Leaves me in a rush.

Temptation
by Marina Ramirez

Almost everywhere you go,
No matter who you see,
You will always be tempted into doing drugs.
You think it's cool,
But what it really does is change you on the inside and out.
It turns you into something no one wants to be around with,
You start to lose yourself to it,
And start becoming this monster.
A monster addicted to money, power,
And even all the drugs you can get your hand on.
You start to push your family and friends away, not wanting to deal with them.
Then you start to lose interest in your sports, hobbies, and school activities.
Each night, before you walk out the door to hang out with all your so-called friends
Who say that they have your back no matter what kind of trouble you are in
Your parents would say to take care of yourself.
Some might think that they are telling you what to do,
But what they are really trying to tell you is to have fun
And yet at the same time, to be careful on how much fun you actually have.
Parents want only the best for you
And not end up hanging out with the wrong people,
Getting killed out in a gang fight out on the street,
Or becoming a parent at a very young age.
Your parents might not know that much about the streets,
But they know a lot more than what you think they do.
It's important to listen to your parents when they tell you something,
Even when you know it's wrong,
And not get too tempted into doing or making all the wrong choices.

The Perfect Girl
by Austin Shin

The girl of my life
Does she really exist or just a part of my dreams?
Now I know the answer but it may be hard to believe
She's in this classroom sitting right beside me.
What would I do without this girl?
The feeling of it just makes me hurl.
I hope I never know the answer to my question
Because some things are just better left alone.
She dances in the rain.
She smiles and laughs.
That's the best thing in the world.
The way she looks, the way she's like
It leaves me speechless and my mouth gaping open
She is the epitome of perfection
With absolutely no exception.
And I wouldn't have asked for anything more.

Apparently She's Perfect
by Olivia Simpson

Apparently she's perfect,
Has all the guys.
Great grades, a pretty smile, sweeter than honey,
She's even pretty funny.
Apparently she's perfect,
I wish I wasn't jealous.
I'm trying hard not to be,
Just isn't easy.
Apparently she's perfect,
Has all the friends in the world.
No wonder why,
She's most definitely not shy.
Apparently she's perfect,
She's really nice and sweet.
I love her to death,
But just wish I could see ...
That no one is perfect,
Not even her.
God loves us all the same,
That's for sure

Baseball
by Lucas Still

Baseball is a terrific sport
That's why it's America's pastime
And I will tell you about it
With this little rhyme
First, the pitcher takes the rubber
And throws a marvelous ball
If the batter does not swing
Then it's the ump who makes the call
But if the batter swings
And takes a superb cut
Then you might hear
A crack louder than a nut
This means the ball was hit
And maybe put in play
If a fielder makes a catch
Everyone shouts "Hurray!"
Baseball has so many elements
That would take too long to tell
But if you go to a ball game
You better be ready to yell!

The Eye of Love
by Nathalia Wallace

Could love truly be that shallow?
In the eye, but not the ear,
In the pants, but not the heart,
Does it even matter what you say or do?
When all they know is what they see,
Through this foggy deep blue.
Make-up and clothes, is that all that it takes?
"Stop talking and start prodding and poking"
But this is not me!
Clothes are but covers to hide the true you,
Make-up; the paint of lies ...
Oh, but can't you see?
What this does to the heart

Life Is Cold
by Andy Welsh

I climbed that morning,
Up a hill covered in snow,
With my kind old friend.
Feeling very queer,
I asked, "Why is it so cold?"
The wind jeered a frosty hug.
I whined, "The top must be near!"
(Life is kind, but quite cold.)
The top slowly appeared.
I spirited there with massive joy!
The mountain snarled icy sneers.
I arrived on top.
But, I descended with fear.
When I tried to bail out,
My friend held me back.
I crashed into a tree.
My old friend still runs the show.
He was kind; now he's shrewish and old.

Crushed
by Sydney Witt

Your eyes, your smile
They're so beautiful.
They make me feel warm inside.
Whenever you're around
It's plain for me to see
That you should be my guy.
I try my best to be on top,
But another is probably there.
I think those other girls look like total ditzes
When they sit and twirl their hair.
I do everything that I can do,
And, boy, is it a lot.
I just hope that you won't shut me out
Before I get my shot.

The Bout
by Nicholas Leibowitz

They step in the ring, each one eager to begin the dance
They wait for the ding, the tension like a cancer
Alas! The bell begins to sing, they rush, each arm a lance
Each fist like a cannon ready to sting, two gladiators waiting for their chance
And then, the bear delivers what he came to bring, the fox is caught at a glance
So he bites back, determined to be the king, and the bear ceases to dance

Ode To Him
by Clara Ratu

Every morning I wake up,
And thoughts of you flow
Into my mind.
You're one of a kind.
A moment spent with you
Is one that I will cherish forever.
We're meant to be together.
Your smile dazzles me
Like a bright summer day.
I hope our love will never fade.
Practically perfect for each other;
You're my puzzle piece.
We fit together with complete ease.

Angel's Voice
by Kaitlyn Rodgers

There was always the voice of an angel in the sweet lullaby of my dreams,
Who would sing me a song that owned the melody of Heaven
That awakened the light in my soul,
The voice sang the rhythm of God's grace that sparked the light within me,
The voice cantillated the majestic song of Heaven
And sang the ever flowing lyrics of peace and hope,
As this voice awakened my soul, I began to realize the eternal beauty of life,
Life is beautiful as years go by and as you take in your breaths,
Life is beautiful as you think the soft thoughts implanted in your mind by emotions,
This angel's mesmerizing voice provided me the knowledge of life
And how precious and delicate it is,
For it was the voice of an angel
That awakened my soul.

Life
by Odessa VanOrder

Life, can be given, can be taken,
Like travelling through
The uneven ridges of
Cracks in tiles of the bathroom floor
In which ants take silent passage,
In which, in an open
Nook or cranny found
In said crack in tile
A queen may lay her eggs;
In it are given lives.
Or as a darkened spider waits in
That same cavernous nook,
Lying patiently in wait;
And as an unsuspecting warrior
Takes a rest, is caught; and the
Spider takes a life
Such can be said for bees and birds and humankind
As fate is both merciful and cruel
It also takes its role in life

Hunting
by Seth Nelson

A little bit ago
I was hunting all day
Sweet anticipation
I just had to sit and stay
As the sun slowly rises
Morning's first cool day breeze
Waiting, watching, hoping
All the while my eyes tease
Just a glimpse and it was gone
Could it quite possibly be
The deer I've been waiting for
Then it made a desperate flee

First Thing I Would Do
by Jon-Luc Heroux

A long time ago
I accepted and started to know you
But then all the fakeness started to press in
If only I knew the real you
Then later I began to see
That you died just for me
This then, took a while to accept
I then saw you with glee
Now I talk and listen to you
Everything I do is consulted by you
If I could go it again
The first thing I would do is accept you

Troubled Itch ...
by Caleb Hoffmann

The feeling has come today,
I feel the bitter patch,
It is inside my nose, I feel that I must scratch.
But all the boys and girls are looking around the room,
Daydreaming, but if they catch me
I just might feel the doom.
So I will play it safe, I shall not misuse, my finger to pick my nose,
I'll get up and use tissues ...

A Winter's Night
by Nikki Shipman

As I walked with thee,
Down the narrow road,
All I could think about,
Was you and all of the cold.
The path that lay ahead,
Was only going to be,
What I always dreamed of,
It was all about me.
You might have thought wrong,
But to me I am right.
As if to say everything,
All I want is a good night

Summer
by Kenzie Medley

Summer: you bring joy to children in the world
Your days are long and very warm
Which makes trips to the lake even more fun
Where people fish, and swim, and ski
But as your weary days drag on
It brings those very unwanted days
For kids must go back to school
And dream of your fun days once more

A Lesson Learned
by Bobbi Reeves

To yourself, always stay true
Live for yourself, don't try to impress
Others may care what you do
But to you, it will always cause stress
Live for the moment; follow your heart
And the ones who love you most will never part

Athlete
by Jarred Coddington

So happy to be a football player.
I fall on the ground and fly in the air.
Being tackled so hard is hard to bear.
But I love when we win, so I don't care.

The Snail Apology
by Enrique Taitt

Snail, snail, so small, so pale,
You cross my garden the night before day.
Snail, snail, so small, so pale,
You leave your silvery streak along my trail.
Snail, snail, so small, so pale,
I did not see you when you crossed my trail.
Snail, snail, so small, so pale,
I crushed you, I killed you, I flattened you like a flake.
Snail, snail, so small, so pale,
Please forgive me for my mistake.

Tall Trees
by Scott Marschner

Trees
Green leaves
They are magnificent
A wonderful
Redwood

How About Today?
by Caitlin Smith

Do you ever feel like you're all alone?
Nothing to feel and no one to hold, nothing that you can call your own.
You sit alone in your room just wondering what went wrong.
Why doesn't anyone see, why don't they ever believe in what you have to say?
Maybe it will come another day.
Nothing will make everything okay.
No! Not somebody, how about now?
How about today?
Please, enough excuses.
Can't you see that we are losing this ...
You yell at me.
I yell at you.
Maybe for one day.
Maybe for two ...
Can't you see that I'm going insane?
Why can't you just see, why don't I explain,
That you and me could never be we.
Why does it have to be like this?
Why does this have to be like the sea, just never-ending;
This needs to end.
I've got to leave.
Can't you see what this is doing to me?
We used to be pals.
We used to be buddies.
Then we gave love a try and we just let it die?
So not someday, no!
Not later ...
How about today?

Nature Attraction
by Laura Sywyk

My mind is full of thoughts and worries
Then I see it, the water elegantly falling ...
So beautiful, so graceful, so enchanting
As it rushes down
Like the water
My thoughts cascade off the precipice of my mind
Leaving nothing but this moment
I hear the rapid water roaring
Yet, like my thoughts, it is completely silent
I taste the crisp air throughout the woods
I smell the moistness, the musty minerals surrounding me
Though it is far away, I have an urge to reach out ...
To feel the frigid water flowing over me
No one can resist the alluring presence of a waterfall

Ode To Summer
by Stephanie Cohn

Oh, summer
You're here at last, someone I've been awaiting
No more homework, no more worries
Time for staying up late, sleeping in till noon
Summer is here, the sun is shining
Birds are chirping, never stopping
I'm in love with the summer breeze
The feel of the leaves, even though you make me sneeze
I love you, summer
The way you make me feel free, you will be here always, and forever
And everyday summer's gone, we'll be waiting.
With one whiff of summer air
The smell of summer grabs me tightly
I'm lost in the heat of the sun, and the cool water that touches my feet.
The memories I make, I'll never forget
I'm lost forever in the wonderful season of summer.

Watching Me
by Gina Somara

One day Daddy came home drunk
He asked for my mother
He shot her seven times, while I hid behind the purple-patterned chair
I was very scared until a transparent man came and cuddled me
The police came, they asked where I hid
I told them, "Behind the purple-patterned chair"
They asked if it was just me
"No," I responded
"Jesus came and cuddled me, didn't you see him?"
A confused "No" responded
Then I saw Him
He floated out the roof, back to Heaven
"See?" I sobbed to them
They didn't see
That's when I realized someone was watching me

In the Mirror
by Haleigh Coburn

I look into the mirror,
I see a mystery.
So many things I can be,
But one passion sings out to me.
Music is my soul.
Deep down my heart screams,
That only the sweet beat of rhythm,
Matters to me.
My life is the tone,
My heart plays the beat,
My soul is the vocals,
That sings out to me.
I look in the mirror,
I find my mystery.
My passion for music,
Sets my soul free.

Boo Radley
by Audrey Vaughan

On a summer day, I think it was sunny,
I was eating soup with animal crackers.
In the corner of the bowl, all alone was a mouse.
On the other side of the bowl was a rat.
And in the middle was a cat.
It seemed as if the cat couldn't figure out which one to go after.
The mouse looked unaware of the issue, naive.
But the rat was very aware, attentive.
Slowly, the rat floated across the bowl
By the cat, to protect the mouse from danger.
But the mouse floated up,
Oblivious to the rat trying to help it.
I welcome the rat, unlike the mouse.
Welcome to our town, Alexandra.

Nature In Yosemite, California
by William Kirby

In Yosemite, there are birds who sing.
There are flowers whose scent can make you nap.
Trees as tall as skyscrapers, and even some trees smell like vanilla.
There are waterfalls that can blow you away with beauty.
Mountains storm the skies with their height.
Climbers look as small as a grain of rice.
There are long trails filled with sweat of others.
There are animals who have hooves, and sharp teeth.
Nature is the definition of Yosemite.

Bees
by Erika Thalman

Bees are busy, buzzy things with the stinger on one end.
Some are skinny, some are fuzzy and some are a blend.
There are so many kinds a bee can be.
It is a very large variety.
Honeybees make sticky honey, and meat bees eat meat.
But I'm not sure why the bumblebee is called the bumblebee.
That is a complete mystery to me.
Perhaps it's because of their movement,
Or they bump into things so much.
But what I'm really trying to say here is that when it comes to bees,
It means a bunch.

Escape
by Ilana Holt

I love the way the wind rushes in my face
As I cross the finish line
And can hardly take a breath
That proud feeling that sits deep in the pit of my stomach
How can anybody hate running
When it makes you feel
So good
So alive
So free
Where all you can think about is the next breath you take
Your pounding heart
And those legs beneath you
Carrying you farther
And farther
And farther
Letting you
Escape

When You Fly
by Melinda Miller

When you fly
You'll leave me behind
When you soar
I'll be next door
When you cry
I'll dry your eyes
When you sing
I'm listening
If you decide to take a dive
I'll be with you at all times
But when you fly
You'll leave me behind
When you fly
You'll fly high
When you fly
Dear, I don't mind
But when you fly
We'll have to say, "Goodbye."

Single Cut
by Kimberly Taketa

Just a prick was all I asked
Just a sliver of blood
Just a moment with tingles
Just a single cut
All I wanted was an escape
All in one prick it spread
All just a physical pain
All for a single cut
More of this peace
More on the arm and legs
More blood craved
More than a single cut
It gives such a rush
It forges my faith
It was more than physical
It was a single cut
In a sleeve it hides
In one cut I smile
In the moment, in my mind
In all, it started with a single cut.

Love Is But a Word
by Madelyn Wilhite

Love is but a word.
You don't really know what it means till you have found the right person.
When you're eight years old and your first crush takes your hand
And says, "I love you." Does he really mean it? Does he even know what love is?
When you're thirteen and your boyfriend says
That you are the most beautiful girl in the world and you are his princess
And he loves you. Does he mean it or is he just saying that
Because he doesn't want to hurt your feelings?
When you're twenty-five and that guy you have been dating for three years
Takes you out to dinner and gets down on one knee and says, "I love you!"
And then you see a beautiful ring. Does he mean it?
When you're sixty-nine and the man you grew up around,
Had your first kiss with, was your high school sweetheart,
Asked your father if he could have your hand in marriage,
And is now the father of your kids ...
When he takes your hand and says, "I love you, babe!"
It's not just a word anymore, it's an action, a belief,
A knowing that he truly does love you and he means it.
Love is not but a word anymore.

The Paradox of a River
by Shivani Mathur

Shimmering like a sheet of silver,
Reawakening with the fresh colors of dawn,
Snaking its way along crevasses and valleys,
A wave here, a droplet there, and gone.
Gentle ripples on the stagnant surface,
A calm breeze fluttering in the air,
A soothing "shh" tune in the wind,
Who controls it? What's in there?
Pulsing to the rhythm of nature,
Using might beyond all measure,
A murky gray is veiled below,
It reveals secrets, emotions, treasures.
The mess of algae undergrowth,
Rocks and pebbles strewn around,
Dirt and blood mingled and tossed,
Loves have been lost, men have been drowned.
For it has a beauty that's haunting, knowledge but brawn,
Upon the surface are gleaming greens, golds, and brass,
Its ugliness is more than can be described in words,
Because the beauty of this river is unsurpassed.

Ode To Shooting Stars
by Vandita Anand

Shining so bright, I only see you once in a while.
One magnificent moonless night
You fall through the sky
As quick as a lightning strike,
I don't even have a chance to blink my eyes.
Shooting around the world, you appear in my sight
With perfect timing.
I wish upon you, hoping my wish will come true
Even though you have a heavy burden
Of wishes to fulfill.
Your beauty lit up the sky
Just like a child's smile lights up
When given a brand new toy.
You become smaller and smaller, fading away.
The sky is a dark and gloomy place to see, without your presence.
Will you please come back for me?

The Star-Spangled Banner
by Arjun Balasingam

On the third of September,
Mr. Francis Scott Key wrote our song,
Which we will remember
Forevermore long.
He was kept aboard the ship,
A part of the British territory.
He longed to get out of this hardship,
While the Americans achieved victory.
Proud of his land,
He composed our song,
Written in short hand,
Yet very strong.
And so we still remember and sing this beautiful paean,
Which originated during the war with the Europeans.

War
by Madison Browning

The soldiers march into battle
Looking death straight in the eye
They hear the pounding of guns
The sounds of the dying
The battle is long
Blood litters the Earth
Adrenaline flows through veins
Man and animal merge into one
Defeated, the enemy turns to flee
But the soldiers are ordered to show no mercy
The deed is done; the soldiers are saved
Still they can't help but think of the ones they have slain
So many innocent, young men
Who lie dead in the dirt
And the soldiers are heartbroken
They did not deserve this
As they march away their eyes become clouded
Crying silent tears for the ones that have fallen
But they know that they will have to be strong
For wherever war goes, death follows along

Sodium
by Hayli Cole

In 1807 I was isolated from the element potassium;
It was Sir Humphry Davy who discovered me.
My sign is "Na," my color is a silvery-white,
I'm light and soft, but dangerous to water.
If water and I get near each other there is sure to be an explosive reaction.
I don't know why but I just can't stand him,
There's just something about the watered down substance that gets to me.
Anyway let me continue. I'm from the alkali metals, the best of them all,
We're soft and fare and we conduct heat and electricity.
Not to brag or be rude but I am the fourth most abundant element.
The stars even love me. Doctors make medicine to help their patients
Out of my brilliant, natural compound. I also help with agriculture
And organic compounds too. Just by looking at my intensive heat
Those molten metals become purified at my feet.
I have so many uses as you can see; it's great to be me.
Now here are some little details about me. My favorite number is eleven,
That's a pretty impressive atomic number to me.
Mass number I believe is twenty-two point nine but let's just say it's 23.
I have twelve neutrons and my density is two-hundred ninety-three.
I absolutely love everything about me, I'm shiny and silvery
And pretty as can be. Life is great to be an element like me.

Tsunami
by Sanika Kulkarni

It was a calm summer morning
I walked along the pebble strewn shore
On the sparkling, green expanse, staring out into the open sea
The boat rocking, the fishes swimming
The shopkeepers opened up their stores
I gripped the fishing pole in my hands, pigeons waddled beside me
They heard it before they saw it, staring transfixed on the beach
The water was having a roaring fit, then it rose from the sea
A menacing green, white-capped wave. It tossed, snarled, crashed, and broke
Only one person remained safe. Staring at the shore, fisherman and his boat

Love and Compassion
by Devyn Young

A heart is but a heart if love and compassion
Do not follow through it.
But if it has love and compassion,
Then the heart shall live forever.
But without it, it is dead before it dies.
Nowadays, compassion is overlooked, as is love.
You are considered a weakling, but really the ones
That have nothing but a heart are weaklings.
For they have no alibi or enforcement
To stand on when they stumble.
But with love and compassion
There is always going to be a rock to stand on.
A heart is ice without love and compassion,
But a strong willful thing with it.

Similar Skies
by Alyssa Glascott

When all clouds gather 'round
Not a shred of light is found
Foolish worries soon forgot
Social battles have been fought
Foul feelings released to show
Heartfelt tears at last let go
The clock is ticking back and forth
South can see the same as North
One returns to a high priced home
Another walks the streets alone
Existing on another side
Eventually the two collide
Light casts a knowing glance
Rays prancing their last dance
Eyes upon their playful game
Sunsets always stay the same

The Man In the Wall
by Zach Coleman

The man in my wall
Watches as I go to school
Watches as I come home
Watches me as I sleep
But, I do know if he is here to help me or hurt me
I feel creepers in my bones
I feel goose bumps in the back of my neck
My hair stands up stiff
In curiosity and crassness

I'm Sorry Revenue
by Angela Cwiklinski

I'm sorry for not spending as much time with you as I should have.
I didn't ride you enough
I didn't groom you enough
I'm sorry I rode all those other horses
And only rode you when someone else couldn't
Or when the little kids did something wrong
I'm sorry I got mad when you bit me
And charged at me in the pasture
Or attacked my friends
I'm sorry I had to let you go
And wasn't there enough on that horrible night
That still haunts me today
I'm sorry I ride other horses now
And that I have a new show horse
And that I have a new partner
Most of all, I'm sorry that we're not together
I love you, and I miss you
You're my best friend and you always will be
Revenue

3rd Place

Lorena Lipe

Lorena attends an all girls Catholic high school
and is a member of a very interesting forensics team.
In her last year at middle school,
this hard working student was awarded the honor of Salutatorian,
and has been recognized by The Who's Who Registry
of Academic Excellence.

Midnight Illusions
by Lorena Lipe

Eyelids flutter like the wings of a butterfly
Adrenaline pumps through veins as heartbeats race to diminish
Large beads of sweat languidly trickle down
And collect at the nape of the neck
Shallow breaths, filled with sighs of relief, are presented before glossy eyes
It was just a dream ...
Head to toe, the body is shielded
Streams of perspiration stain the comforter,
Yet the body quivers with fearful expectations
An unidentified noise bathes the room with ominous sounds
A yelp escapes the mouth, and a pulse throbs
It was just a dream
Shadows paint the walls as a candle flickers in the corner
Porcelain toes warily touch the ground,
As long legs move stealthily across the bare floor
The wind intruding from the window whispers warnings,
And kisses the vulnerable flesh
Tapered fingers tightly wrap around the doorknob
Sharply pulled, a heavenly light is exposed
The melancholy ambience is washed with relief
It was just a dream

2nd Place

Helena Rainville

Helena fancies herself an adventurer.
Whether it's starting her first year at high school
or traveling the world after graduation,
she is always looking forward to new experiences.
Reading and writing are two of her favorite pastimes,
but she also enjoys sports,
especially field hockey.

An Artist's View
by Helena Rainville

A splotch of paint
On canvas, white,
An insignificant form in the world.
A small speck of the brush's
Independent thought.
Nothing more was done.
For nothing needed to be.
Many looked and wondered.
What could this be?
A boy saw a dragon,
A mother saw a child,
A teacher saw a number,
And then the artist looked,
And smiled.
Imagination was the key.

1st Place

Jeremiah Rogers

Jeremiah is a very talented author
who enjoys going to church and attending school
where he is a member of the Latin Club.
His Christian faith is what's most important to him,
and he believes in speaking his mind.
His love for poetry runs deep
as does his creative writing ability.

Hot Hell
by Jeremiah Rogers

As she stepped into the room,
I inhaled the cinder and ash on her skin.
Her hair raged as a great forest fire,
Black with red streaks, and just a wisp of bleached white.
Her eyes were the color of cherry oak firewood,
One with just a spark of flame left.
Her lips were glossed with kerosene,
And with a kiss, set me on fire.
The dress flared bright red,
A flame begging for blood.
I fell in love with this burning fire.
She scorched my heart.
Consuming it to the last vessel.
But, there's a spark where my heart used to be
And it will always live on.

Division IV

Grades
10-12

Illusion of Love
by Jose Ojeda

Would I or would I not compare my love and darkness?
My heart is full of cold ice
I've had enough of this heart being heartless
But this piece of organ has a price
And all it was, was your warmth and worthiness
And tasted love like it was a spice
The closer I got to you, I sensed coldness
You betrayed me and told lies
I cried all night and felt a warm hug with happiness
It was you holding me because you heard my cries
While you were holding me, in a few seconds I felt lifeless
I have two questions before I leave
Why did you stab me twice?
And why are you so full of darkness?
All I heard from you was, "I had no kindness ... "

A Gift From God
by Claire Roca

The way the lights hits your eyes
When you smile
The innocence of your laugh
And your joy
Your kindred nature, loving touch
I am thankful for you.
The glistening of your cheeks
When tear stained
The whimper of your lips
And your cry
Your fragile body, tender soul
I am here for you.
The way you see the good
When I'm hurt
The gentle look on your face
When I cry
Your perfect being, warm embrace
I love you.

Emily
by Ashley Killeen

I spent time searching for someone like you,
Who laughs and smiles, your happiness always true.
Your smile brought sunshine on the worst of days,
Your laughter built paths that showed us the way.
You lived to ski and skied with such grace,
We saw your love for the sport at every race.
You were a friend, a sister, a daughter, and so much more,
You are loved by everyone who knew you and your passion for life we adore.
And even though you are gone,
We still stand in your sunshine and follow your paths.
We want you to know you will always be in our hearts,
With all of our memories, it won't seem like we are apart.
Every day I think about what we've been through,
And I'm so very thankful my searching lead me to you.

Love Sick
by Melcher Batangan

Because baby, you're the one I see
In this full movie of what is to be called picture perfect ...
Now you're gone and you remain only as a memory
Imperfection that stains my mind,
I'm too inclined to say that it's time
To let go of the flowers and feathers,
I float above the clear blue sky
Because every time looking into your eyes
I melt away into heavenly gasp
You made me bloom as the spring came,
It's too bad to say that we didn't last
Never had the thoughts of procrastination
Only the time to kill, but the drink spilled
Our last toast to sip, and one last kiss
I never shared a bliss like this
As the time keeps at ticks, and I remain for the heavenly Miss
I stay up knowing that my days turned to nights
But my nights never turned to days,
It's essential that I must have you to survive this desperation
Is this the ends of where we meet
A final destination that ones must restrict,
If so let the love lament away into the air
Of what we might breath again as time goes by,
But for now let my soul fly away
I remain a mystery to your eyes that you soon start to gaze

Cleansed
by Raven Sisco

Here I am, warm between toes,
With ocean foam tickling them.
Moist droplets hug my ankles,
As tide tugs water back to sea.
Here I am, salt clinging to lips.
Breezes sigh, caressing my face.
Sunlight dances on my skin,
As I stretch arms toward Heaven.
Here I am, surrounded by water,
To knees, waist, then shoulders.
I open myself and let the ocean
Wrap me in an aquatic embrace.
Here I am, floating on my back,
With gulls jetting across the sky,
I listen as they call to one another.
Aqua sea rinses my thoughts away.

Who Thee Is
by Mayra Rodriquez

I am from Antonio, Maria, Antonio and many more,
From grape smelling wineries,
From overflowing rivers
I am from pozole, tamales, and carne asada eaters
I am from funny, alcoholic, and humorous
From hardworking labor men,
From, "Come on, you go get it; you're younger"
I am from honesty, sincerity, politeness, and kindness.
I am from the Lion King to Lassie
I am from Mysty, Cookie and Oso
I am from the always losing Raiders.
I am from Stephanie Myers to Hoops authors
From the smartness to the foulness
From the popular to the unpopular
From the neatness to the sloppiness
I am from the great land of the roses
This, if you shall ask, is what makes me.

I'm
by Sara Bayles

I'm lonely.
I'm sad.
I'm pathetic.
I'm mad.
I'm empty.
I'm cold.
I'm crazy.
I'm alone.
I'm anxious.
I'm numb.
I'm waiting.
I'm coming undone.
This is what you've done to me!
You break me in half.
But the past is the past
And there's no turning back.
My life is full of regrets I try constantly to hide.
I lie in my hollow bed and cry into the night.
Why?
Why did you let this happen to me?
Why do you laugh as I lay here and bleed?
But when the tears have fallen and my heart is faded away,
I close my eyes and dream of a much better day.
I pray for an escape–someone to save me and set me free.
Someone just to love me.
I beg of you–please!

Mask
by Megan McMillan

There is a girl who wears a mask.
She always wears the mask around her friends.
Sometimes she forgets to take the mask off.
Sometimes she forgets to put the mask on.
This mask hides all the humiliation that she has put up with.
This mask hides all the pain and the suffering in her life.
She wears the mask because she is afraid of what her friends might think.
She wears it to be a new person.
I am the girl that wears the mask.
I forget to take the mask off and put it back on.
I am the girl that hides humiliation, pain, and suffering with a mask.
I am a girl that wears a mask because I'm afraid of what my friends will think.
I wear the mask so I can be a different person.

Recognition of Love
by Ryan Houlihan

From the first time our eyes linked
There was a spark that lit a fire
Butterflies flew throughout my body
Nothing can change the connection of my desire
Chemistry rages through the electric charge of love
The soul's recognition was found
True love was floating upon air
Waiting, wanting to be bound
At the moment you find love
Hold tight to it. Keep her close to your heart
Dream of the possibilities you and she can make
For true love can never keep you apart

My Boyfriend
by Tyana Williams

My boyfriend's name is Steven;
He brings me happiness in every season,
Despite our stupid fights,
We can look at each other with the biggest delight.
He brings me sunshine like a sunflower,
It's amazing how he has that power
I call him my baby,
I call him my boo,
Who's to say that we can't get married real soon?
He brings me faith and he brings me hope,
Dang, if I were to leave him, I'd be a stupid dope
I love him with all my heart, I love him so much,
And if people don't like it, then they can just shut up!

Your Voice
by Morgan Petersen

Your voice is music to my ears.
The kind of song you hear,
And know everything will be alright.
When my world comes crashing down,
Your voice is the one I want to hear.
It's like that song you have memorized.
The song that's your lullaby.
That encouraging, inspiring song you listen to when you're feeling down.
The sweetness in your voice I hear is mine.

Planet of Freaks
by Arika McGuire

I am a freak that walks this planet
Bound by an unseen chain
My thoughts are melting into nothing
Some days I go insane
I cannot say what's in my heart
Or what is in my brain
I am a freak that walks this planet
Living in constant pain
I am a freak that walks this planet
With voices ringing in my ears
The pounding inside my head
Of a million terrifying fears
Others may see me as a loser,
But one thing is clear
I am a freak that walks this planet
And things are not as they appear.

Freedom Don't Come Easy
by Jeffrey Grissom

Freedom to me is like life, you want to have a good life
But just don't know what is going to happen in life
For me, people keep talking and won't stop it seems
In life I cannot find freedom
But a person in my life who has stuck by me
Through the good days and the bad days
Is one of my good, good friends
And that person is Trey Hill, 14, one of my best friends.
I told Trey one day that if nobody in the whole world had faith in me,
I need you, and he will always be my friend
And if there is another person in my life who has been close to me
It is a guy named Zadren Wright, 3
One day we played a football game and he had two TDs
I hoped to play tightend last season and I didn't
And I didn't play that game, and I was thinking I was never going to play again
I thought it was just me, but Z told me some real stuff that night
I was crying like a newborn baby, but he said Juicy was wrong
And I said I didn't play tonight, and I felt sad
But Z said that he loved me, and I won't forget that night
To me, freedom don't come easy.

I Am From
by Jasmine Mendoza

I am from
Ruth Marie Cordova and Harvey Hopkins,
Ardive Ruth Cazares and Antonio Petez Cazares,
Ana Blue-Sky Aguilera,
I am from
The rocky mountains of California,
From the loud streets, busy roads,
And paleta stands of Santa Rosa.
From long, dusty trails of Michoacán, Mexico.
From the salty and cold waters of the ocean and river.
I am from
Strong and beautiful Spain.
I am from greasy fried bread, salty seaweed, hot and spicy tamales,
Warm burritos, and succulent abalone eaters.
I am from
A stubborn, noisy, loud,
And opinionated working-class family.
I am from
What created me, from what my great nation
Shaped me into what I am today.

The Way You Paint Me
by Alexa Adams

You could paint me black,
Or you could paint me white,
Or the color of the sea
On a stormy night.
These colors don't describe me;
Only who I am to you.
What I am on the outside
Doesn't bare my soul to you.
Don't paint me for who I was,
Or who I might have been.
My past is long gone;
I've been washed of my sin.
Paint me for who I am
And who I want to be.
Paint me in all my colors,
For all the world to see.

Love Divided
by Katrina Soliday

As I gaze into your eyes,
The only thing I see are your lies.
Somehow your spells put me in a trance,
But no more of this forgotten romance.
So many friends; I have only a few,
I long to be someone new.
I can't help but remember all the times we had,
And when I think of these things it makes me sad.
It was a love divided at the seams,
A love so big you could imagine it in your dreams.

Mistake
by Wanda Stephens

Addictive cancer I have seen you take pieces of my life,
My heart–like a handsome black hole
Gleaming teeth, a Cheshire smile,
Swallow innocence with the kisses of experience and darkened delight
But where seduction has ended, destruction begins
A peculiar sound of laughing animosity
Once mesmerized by red chords,
Now victimized by internal images and romantic expectations
That agonizing voice whispers in my mind, a wisdom learned in doubt,
Do not awaken love until the time is right
Knowledge received only after the fruit of the seed, rots inside a broken heart

Time
by Taylor Stroud

Sometimes I look up into the sky
It reminds me of the past
Then I start to cry
I can feel the wind
Like dolphins swimming through water
I know I have sinned
But time keeps going on
Like buffalo on the prairie
Then I walk out on the lawn
I can smell the sweet smell of spring
As sweet as honeysuckle
When I think of time, I sing

A Man With a Gun
by Masin Sharp

I heard a silent scream of the girl next door
So I walked in the room and saw her on the floor
I crept up to her and asked, "What's wrong?"
She told me her hair was too long
Then I heard a silent blast from outside
A few seconds later I saw a man who cried
Someone had shot a man with a gun
He was drunk and he thought he was having fun
Now as he sits in this bright obscurity
Because of this, he has thoughts of insecurity
So the only thing he knows to do, is get a clue
But the problem is he still doesn't know what to do
So he keeps on the couch to be a silent bomb
He can't think of what to do, but call his mom
She's in shock; he just realized he's off to jail
That man decided to go out shooting, but, oh well

My Absolute Masters
by Julio Damian

I close my eyes and I still see you deep inside my own skin ...
You penetrate me, with your soul you penetrate me,
For it's a delusion that to lives manifest.
It holds hands with time and I let him with his strange steps take me to remember;
My childhood and my life which shall never be mine again,
For you now own them in each and every sense.
I stare at my past, my truth;
For look at me now, you who can realize what I've lost in each of those years.
It says nothing, your mouth says nothing ...
And in every attempt we both must but lose, because who are our eyes say it all.
We lose, to the world we both lose ...
Although even He can't imagine we both exist now,
And everything is nothing to defeat us.
You stare at me, with more than your eyes you stare at me ...
Knowing that with every glance I can die with such a beauty.
What happens, you tell me what happens,
Because I don't understand, and much less should humanity.
What happens, tell me what happens,
Because our own reflection agonizes with every glance in its own mirror,
If it is them, those two eyes who call themselves ... My absolute masters?

Death
by Kellie Beasley

It glistened in the moonlight,
Charging at me,
Like an animal,
Hungry for death,
All that's left is a pool of blood,
There will be tears,
No one will ever find me.

Wish
by Tesia Carney

To my newborn cousin, little Brea, so tiny, fragile and new
Sleeping in your bed with my baby blanket spread across you,
Listening to the same music I do
While sleeping so sound,
It's amazing how someone so young can make me feel so proud
Sitting here watching, I can't help but know
That these precious moments will go by oh–so–fast
So, as you grow and learn things meant only for you,
Here is my single gift I give to you, of all the things I wish for you
I wish that you would love life and enjoy every minute of it,
That you would learn to love, and know when to give it,
That the things in life which make you glad
Would vastly outnumber those that make you sad
I wish that, no matter what happens, you would make the most of it
Even when you feel as though you're in the worst of it,
Little girl, become patient and wise
Don't ever try to disguise who you really are
Only then, will you quicker be,
All that you were meant to be
Some things to remember, little girl
Like me, you are the first, and therefore the most spoiled!
Being firstborn though, won't always be easy!
You're the one who will teach your mom and dad to be all that they can be
You're so precious, child; more beautiful than the largest rose!
You'll grow up, and we won't let you go
We love you, Brea, we truly do
And out of all the things I wish for you ,
The one wish that rings the most true, is that you love us forever,
And we will too
–Written on April 1, 2010, for a very special girl. We love you Brea!

Leap of Faith
by Alexander Fergadir

I take the giant leap
I'm scared because the fall is very deep
As I soar through the air I think,
"What happens if my parachute happens to break?"
I finally reach the point of release
The farthest thing I'm from is peace
But then I see the colored umbrella fly
And I become at ease knowing I won't die
Falling, floating slowly to the ground
People greet me and gather all around.

If I Told You ...
by Leann James

If I told you that I had a baby,
What would you say?
Would you embrace me and help me out,
Or just turn me away?
If I told you I was struggling
With drugs and alcohol,
Would you help me get over it?
Or stand and watch me fall?
If I told you I was abused
By a father who drank too much beer,
Would you come and save me from him,
Or leave me to get hurt here?
You don't have to worry.
This has not happened to me.
But, it's happened to many girls
Who still had much to see.
Some wanted to go to college.
Some wanted to finish twelfth grade.
But they couldn't do that,
Because of the choices that had been made.
They weren't able to have fun,
Growing from girls to women.
They had more important things to do,
Like take care of their children.
Unlike those girls, whose decisions were lost,
My whole life is in front of me.
I am still able to choose
Whatever I want to be.

Silly Me
by Robby Knight

I put down my book,
And cast my hook.
Pulled down my hat,
And took a nap.
I opened my eyes,and to my surprise
I can see nothing but dark skies.
Scared I was, all because
That's what the night time does.
Up I stood,
Didn't think I could.
My first step was no good.
Wet as can be,
Up to my knee,
But now ... I can see
I left my hat on,
Silly me!

Shoot For the Stars
by Terra Collins

I know it's hard
But you know,
If you keep moving
Strongly so,
Where you end up
Just might surprise you.
Moving and moving
With much to go through
I know you're hurt,
But don't worry
Try not to think too much
And don't hurry.
If you keep going
And moving on
Then surely your spirit
Will never be gone.
So far,
But if you shoot for the stars
No matter where or how far
It helps make up who you are.

Seasons
by Amalia Borchers

The sun shines bright.
The air is warm and light.
I hear a shout.
Kids run and play about.
Car pools are arranged,
As the air begins to change.
Off to school we head
While the leaves turn yellow and red.
Then cold breezes blow
And fireplaces glow.
Scarves and gloves appear,
As rain drips white instead of clear.
Hope returns and it is seen,
That life blooms and trees green
Snow changes into rain.
We slow our pace and peace we gain.
The cycle is complete.
This, thank God, will repeat.
Seasons come and go,
As an ever changing show.

My Life
by Charleston Grissom

On a cold winter day in January, the fourteenth to be exact
A little baby was born, that baby boy was me, Charleston Ray Grissom
I can't remember how tall I was, but I weighed in at about ten pounds
My momma said I was a big baby at birth
As the years went by I got bigger and bigger and taller
One year at Christmas time, I got a rocking horse
My grandpa bought it for me
I got other gifts, like a cowboy hat, little cowboy boots and a toy gun
But none of those gifts came close to being my favorite as my rocking horse
Years and years and mo' years went by
And those years have changed me to a young man
I'm eighteen now, I'm six feet, two inches tall, and weigh over two hundred pounds
This is not all of my life, but a little taste that I have shared with y'all
So much more to come ...

I Can't Care
by Jordan Rogers

Windy rain
I feel insane
How can you not feel my pain
No sleep
No, not for me
Too scared because of you being
In my dreams.
Day by day
I try and I try
But it seems the more I think
The more I cry
I can't be happy
It's possible, they say
But I'm still sitting here
Waiting for you to even say hey
I'm just going to give up
You're pathetic and don't
Deserve my love.

Life
by Sylvia Welch

Wake up in the mornin'
See the sun turnin'
Moon goin' down
Sun shinin' around
Off to work
Monday morning
Weekend's over
Storming begins
Boss is a jerk
Getting off of work
Time to go home
Kids bouncing around
Time to settle down
Sun is setting
Moon is rising
Stars shining
Bed time arriving.

Untitled
by Jasmine Smith

Why do I feel discourage?
It feels like it's not the Russians in suffrage
I've lost my way
Every day seems like it's not my day
I feel like an unhappy clown
My life is just turned upside down
I'm trapped in a cage
I just wish somebody could just turn the page
I'm sad, mad, glad, bad
This makes me feel like an old wage
I don't have the courage
I don't even have a word for it
All I want to say is suck like
That's what John Ceina says
But when he says "You can't see me"
People really don't feel me

Womb/Heaven
by Tommy Palomino

Helpless in a realm of my own.
This place, dark, wet and small
Is what I have always recognized as home.
I believed I was safe inside this orb,
However outside influence had its way.
Yet I still don't see why I must die.
An aborted thought, an aborted dream
Given up for a distorted freedom.
Conforming to an ignorant train of thought, not of my own.
This sphere of life has quickly become that of chaos and death.
The voice that comforted me for so long
Is the same one I hear asking the doctor, "Will it hurt?"
Created by a hateful God,
I have become a wasted angel,
Killed by my own hate.

If Only I Knew
by Avery Seekford

If only I knew it would be the last time you told me you loved me,
I would have told you 1000 more times before that.
If only I knew it would be the last time I would kiss you,
I would have kissed you 1000 more times before that.
If only I knew it would be the last time you held my hand,
I wouldn't have let go.
If only I knew nothing would ever be the same,
I wouldn't have tried to forget so fast.
If only I knew how much it would hurt,
I would have braced myself for it.
I love you dearly

The Proud
by Kendrick Smith II

Who is that
Who is walking tall
Who wears the hat
Who never falls
The ones who serve
Time after time
Who never observed
The word or rhyme
Watch the tons
Who left their women
Not for fun
For a new beginning
Watch the ones
Who call themselves proud
Who have begun
To hear a sound
For they have won
So they are very loud
They will have fun
'Cause they call themselves proud

Distress of a Vampire
by Robert Bare

Is this desire, to feast
Upon blasphemous human flesh?
To feed this eternal hunger,
To fill the pit of my self-existence.
I would feel guilt,
But my desires take over
For the kill. Forget my morals;
I've lost my rational thought
For the pains will come
Withering away as they watch
He laughs; knows I will give in
Eventually I must overcome
All my mortal thoughts
To fill the pit of my self-existence.

Black
by Alicia Morris

When you look at me, what do you see?
Do you see the color of my skin in which I was born in?
Or do you see a strong African American woman.
My race has become known for the color black when really our skin is brown
Still put down by the prejudice words spoken from others.
I pray to the Lord, humble each day
And ask him to forgive me for the anger I feel
See this reality is unreal, as the words spoken from M.L.K. become forgotten ...
I'm still dreaming what he dreamed as my dignity is torn away from me,
Discrimination each day, flowing this and that way, with the words people say...
Comments like: "You just a ghetto black girl"
Or, "Girl you black I know you can dance"
Or, "I'm not racist I have two black friends"
Well, I don't give a care ... how many "Black" friends you have
Are those supposed to be compliments?
Do we take them as compliments, no we do not!
Because that is not who we are, that is not what I am ...
I am a strong African American woman
Who is proud of her race; those who can relate, don't generate hate,
For the pages of our history will not be ... erased.
We will always remember ...

Fearful Reflections
by Nikki Resendez

If you look too closely into the mirror,
You might just see the thing you fear:
The sunken devil with eyes deep black,
Staring cold, staring back.
You might see all your little mistakes,
Those times you were harsh, those times you were fake.
You might see a face lined with regret,
For the things you'll never be, never do, never get.
You might see a sadness so powerful and raw
That it causes you to step back, trip, and fall.
But the worst thing in a mirror that a person ever saw,
Was nothing, nothing, nothing at all.
You can stare into the mirror and see an empty face,
Not a drop of hope, but a puddle of disgrace.
You can stare at the mirror without a slither of fight,
Or you can back away and make things right.

Broken
by Madeline Roberts

Although you hate me,
What I see
Is not at all an enemy.
But a girl who has been broken,
Beaten and outspoken.
Tough on the outside.
Weak on the inside.
You're not what you claim to be.
I see a girl being used,
Verbally abused
A stupid boy, a cruel father,
Fake friends.
Broken home, broken life.
How have you lived in this strife?
All I can do is pray for you
And this I will never tell:
That even though you scare me,
I'm sorry.
And I know your life is hell.

Fluid Motion
by David Schneider

What would it be like to be the rain
Falling from the sky only to rise again
To be so small then to flow into the ocean
Constantly growing the most fluid motion
Or to be a mountain touching the sky
To be covered with all the plants and life
To hold the tallest trees and smallest pebble
Eternally towering over the horizon
To be a star in the endless universe
To be larger than life, yet seem so small
To see and be seen but to never speak
Forever lighting the night sky
What would it be like to be the wind
In and around everything, yet never seen
To touch the lives of the entire world
To live in the moment, but last forever

A Broken Wing
by Kaci Mcclure

When a baby bird is learning to fly
It sometimes falls from the nest
It screams in pain for its mother's help
No matter hard she tries
She cannot help it
The baby bird will die
Unless someone comes along and helps it
It takes time for the baby bird to try to fly again
When a child is getting beaten
It does not understand what it did wrong
It screams in pain for mercy
No matter how hard the mother tries
She cannot help it
The child will die
Unless someone comes along and helps it
Time can only build trust from a child to its mother or father

High School
by Savannah Sisk

Once you've walked through the glass doors,
Making it down the hall through the crowd
You've been judged by how you look before you can say one word.
Who do you talk to?
What do you say?
How do you act?
Eight classes and two hundred students,
Someone takes you under their wings and now you've a best friend.
The time goes by and things seem to be going wonderful,
And you squander for something to happen.
Your boyfriend becomes a jerk,
You fight and cry every night, drowning in your own tears.
Wishing it would just end.
Friends start changing and they aren't the same any longer.
Pulling apart from each other as ya'll get weaker and the worst becomes stronger.
Stressing over everything,
Am I going to survive this?
This is high school!

Modern Age Youth
by Anthony So

Pressure is what you live with,
Staring at the illuminated whites.
The benefits are established myth.
Boiling acid coming up, sith
You feel that it is what you live with.
The frustration hits you in the pith.
Staying up through the nights,
Even though the benefits are myth.
Disappointment among your kith,
Is the true pain within your sights.
Pressure is what you live with.
You try to get to that zenith,
But the acid is coming up with might.
The drive is the hoping of your monolith.
Your life can go to decay,
Or to some great height if you may;
However, pressure is what you live with,
And the benefits are established myth.

Untitled
by Kirstyn Willis

I see your face
And my heart begins to flutter.
I start to talk
But my words begin to stutter.
I try to walk away
But my feet refuse to lift.
I try to turn my head
But my eyes refuse to shift.
You turn to leave
And my heart begins to break.
My days are numbered
With every breath I take.

The Definition: Love
by Cherie Washington

Love is not something that you can just find, claim, and call yours.
It finds you, claims you, and consumes you as its own.
Any feeling that you have and cannot explain genuinely with your heart is not love.
You could just as easily be feeling lust.
Love is not a game that you play until you're tired
And then you just throw it away when you're finished.
It takes time and devotion to obtain real love.
Love isn't just a physical connection between two people
It is a whole lot more than that.
A bond or connection that can never be broken, that's true love.

The Lake of Tears
by Galen Webb

Things were bad, my grandma cried,
There was a lake of tears between she and I.
I crossed this lake in sad dismay,
And when I get there, I see shades of gray.
There she stood in silence crying,
I walk over, not even sighing.
She looks down at me, I up at her,
Then we hug, and she stops crying, I'm sure
When she does, a rainbow appears,
For when my grandma stops the lake of tears.

Vicarious Fantasy
by Shanteni Wyatt

The sun skipped across her face
As she sat on an aged tree stump
She watched the lush green hills roll
Across the bright orange sky
Birds flew overhead and rustled the leaves
They swooped swiftly to the ground
Pecking at the soft dirt for a quick snack
She curled a long strand of blonde hair around her slender finger
And stared off into the distance
The trees groaned and swayed
Against the slow breeze
Her hair whipped across her face
Blinding her from the beauty of the scenery
She dangled her feet into the clear blue water
Rippling her reflection but cooling her tiny pink toes
Suddenly she heard her name being called
Running towards the voice, she's shaken
Opening her eyes, she sees the desks and books about her
Studious eyes stare at the words on the board
She grins and lays her head back down on the desk.

The Power of Hope
by Nathan Van Ryn

Hope is a thing that can't be bought,
Should not be fought, and is never forgot.
All of us need it, never doubting we are wrong,
Hope keeps us going, it is unshakable and strong
Whether we are hoping for sun all day,
Or for that special someone to stay.
Maybe you hope to someday be a little stronger,
Or ride your bike for just a little bit longer.
Hope is not just a feeling or emotion,
It is what holds us together, it is a devotion
To the prayers for those in need,
Or for an end to jealousy and greed,
Or for your aunt who struggles to go on,
As her cancer comes back when we thought it had gone.
I hope that she can remain strong and tall,
Even when the doctors take her arm, shoulder and all.
How we do it, I really can't say,
But our hope has helped us greet another day.

Lost Not Found
by Malie Sailor

Broken homes,
Torn up streets,
Parks and benches
Where people sleep.
People that beg for change,
Gypsies that play their games.
Little ones that lose their way,
Some go to Heaven,
Some go to gangs.
These streets never sleep.
If the sidewalks could talk,
They might say,
"Help Me!"

A Lucid Dream
by Corben Hudson

I dreamed I walked through the park
And listened to the birds sing a song of chirps.
A house drew closer as if on a conveyor
And I could feel the cool breeze of the air puffing on my face.
The snow numbed my feet with coldness
But somehow I felt at peace.
It was a place of no pain of any kind
People did not even know the words violent, hurt or disgrace.
The sky was clear and the sun shined like an eye of a daisy in the sky
Upon the Earth and its inhabitants.
The mountains appeared as though all you had to do
Was stretch out your arm to feel their beauty and a sloping place.
After awhile, the snow bowed and ran away from before the sun
Enveloping my frozen feet and flowing down the streets
But I didn't care, after all, I was in a dream-like world of silk and lace.

Superhero
by Barbara Beggs

You could be my superhero,
The one I've been waiting for.
To sweep me off my feet,
When I need you the most.
You're the one,
I've been dreaming of.
I stopped dreaming
And you're still here.
My heartbeat goes faster.
I want you closer.
I can't get enough of you.
Having you here,
Makes me happier everyday.
You're the only superhero
I'll ever need.
No one can be compared to you,
Far as I know of.
No one can beat you.
You're my only superhero!

The Raven
by Keosha Chambers

Raven. Raven. Raven.
Sitting in your haven.
What keeps you waiting?
Don't you know? Death's been taken.
I killed him in the evening,
When twilight was gleaming.
He suffered no pain, except for the screaming.
His blood ran, blackening my hands.
I took his bony fingers in my palms,
And swore the forsaken;
Making a sacred oath in night's naked.
I smiled then, lifting his dark veil.
Death grinned; he a she.
Showing he was me.
Raven. Raven. Raven.
Sitting in your haven.
Why are you waiting?

Pieces of You
by Nicole Clement

I won't say goodbye,
What's the point?
I'll see you soon.
You may not be here, bone and joint.
But I know you're higher than the moon.
I won't say goodbye,
I know you're with me each and every day,
Protecting me from what comes my way.
I won't say goodbye,
Because you're with me all the time.
Sharing every moment of clarity and confusion,
Right by my side.
I'm glad to call you mine,
Pieces of you that I combine.
You're gone, this I know.
But I won't say goodbye.

–Dedicated to my family.
We lost my father in 2007
And I hope these words bring my family clarity
As they for me while I was writing.

Stockton, Set Me Free
by Lissette Rodriguez

Since childhood I have said I must leave
That this town offers nothing but hardship.
I want to abandon this life with ease,
Move and never make a homecoming trip.
Stockton has blanketed me with a fear
Not offering me warmth, more-so constraint.
Poverty threatens livelihood, brings tears.
The existence of a hope grows more faint.
Yet as my time rapidly nears to part,
I feel that I leave all of me behind.
My town gives aspiration, a dear art
Love paints a portrait of family binds.
As the world opens up for me to see
I must thank Stockton for letting me free.

Perfection
by Aaron Robinson

Perfection is something we all want,
But can never really achieve.
The wise seek it,
But know it is beyond their reach.
Yet, the foolish think they have already obtained it.
From the married couple arguing their life away,
To the rich man who has nothing better to do
Than watch the chaos that happens in the world so far beneath him.
Nothing is truly perfect.

Daydream
by KenDrell Collins

There was a boy who laid down one night to sleep
As he slept he dreamed of what he would like to be,
He dreamed of being and astronaut. Zoom! Shooting for the stars
He dreamed of going to Jupiter, Saturn, Uranus, and maybe even Mars
He dreamed of climbing a great mountain,
And as a fish drinking from life's great fountain
Of course he dreamed of playing pro-baseball, hitting one out of the park
He dreamed of many things because he wanted to make his mark
He could smell the aroma of sweet success
As he dreamed of acing every test
But morning came and he awoke to sadly see,
All his dreams were merely vanity
Now there was another young man who dreamed a dream or two,
But his eyes were not closed, it was broad day and the sky glowed blue
He had dreams to change the world for you and me
Unlike the other boy, his vision he could clearly see,
And pursue it with great passion,
As a model and her fashion
Him we like to call a 'daydreamer,' one who does not get much sleep
Because he has outstanding goals that must be reached
Like an eagle he does fly
With wings of knowledge and ideas that soar high
Without 'sleep-talking' his words were loudly spoken,
All because he dreamed with his eyes wide open

An Insomniac, Your Honor
by Rachel Cooper

Here, as we "mourn and yet exult"
For the dead who are not dead too young
I am guilty of not sleeping
Guilty of forgetting names and avoiding faces
I am thinking of sin and songs and how I will pay for art school
And I am guilty of not talking
I am missing the living left home in my bed
As I am missing the dead left in the grave
And I am guilty of not sleeping
But how can I sleep when you
Refused to wake?
What can I say when you
Won't speak?
You? You are guilty just like me
But you were found innocent
And you were found dead
But I am guilty of living, and of not talking
And of not sleeping

Moving On
by Evan Robinson

Minutes of silence, hours of weakness
My life flashes before my eyes.
Thousands of tears I have cried.
Celestial arms open and call me up.
My tears surround me, my tears have drowned me.
The voices are here, longing in my head,
In copious ways, they surround me and alarm me that I am dead.
I see my grandpa whom I have missed
He tells me to go back, for there are experiences I will surely miss.
As I head back into my life I wonder about these powerful experiences
And the gilded road that leads the way.
If forever I was to be here, then forever I was to stay,
But, forever was waiting for me, always within my grasp.
Forever was always watching as I slowly tried.
I was the one who had to wait and surely had to stay.
The only thing in my way was that I am meant to stay.
Try as I might and as I want
Like a shining beacon for all.
For this is the path that was set for me.
A path where I must lead the way.

My Superhero
by Jonathan Denney

I am the one who always looks up to you, even still
The one who always would imitate and talk about you like a superhero,
Maybe because you were the one who made me feel like a superhero
I was the one who always volunteered to get your water and tea,
The one who didn't care what you looked like
Because our love was strong, unconditional
I was the one who always made you as characters on video games, remember?
The one who always asked you how to spell "Kevloc", with a C
I am the one who hears your name as it brings back our memories
I am the one little brother you had, still have, and always will
The one who remembers you every day,
And sometimes cries like you were gone just yesterday
I am the one who will eventually meet you again one day

Wetless Tears
by Angelica Holloway

If you could feel how I feel, you would understand my sorrow.
If you could see the things I see, you would understand what I am thinking.
As I know you will never know all the insanity I have endured.
All the unbearable memories I try to forget.
I would never want you to see inside my head. Afraid that you to would disappear.
Clouds of fog pour in on my face, and my eyes start stinging.
The drops of my body rain drips onto my pillow.
I shudder at my concrete torturous future.
Trying not to let the world hear my cries like thunder.
So I seal them inside my throat with invisible tape over my mouth.
I pretend that your comfort is going to use.
That is only because I let you think that I am fine.
A trick only to be pulled off if I cry dry tears. The ones no one can see.
No one can hear them form a puddle under my feet.
Though transparent, they are there like ghost. Haunting me invisibly.
Oh the endless melancholy. So you can not possibly understand my sorrow.
You can not understand my thinking, I will not let you.
You can whine and claim unfairness all you want.
Try to realize that I am trying to protect you.
If you decide to give up and walk away,
All I can say is that it is probably for your own good.
If you decide to stay and be with me,
You just have to know that my wet-less tears will stay and taunt me.

Heart of Prohibited Love
by Lakan Young

Someday an angel will carry my heart to you, when at last, love is legal
Someday our tears will cease to fall, for now our eyes are redder than blood
No longer will it look like a heart, for it has been thrashed around and torn in pieces
No longer will it struggle to beat, but pump blood for both you and I
My lungs, once strong, now wilt in pain
My heart, beating its last painful beats, quivers at the sound of your name
I long to see you, hold you, feel your strong heart giving you life
I know you've suffered too, and the love that we have is prohibited by law
Your face agonized with pain shows me your sincerity
Your bloody wounds spilling out love for me, fighting for what we could have
My lips long to meet yours, like soft rain on a summer's day falling on a red rose
My hands long to hold yours, tighter than the space between two chemical bonds
Even though I am held down in chains, love will set us free
Even though your wings are broken, may I spill my blood and mend them for you
Your broken bones shatter more every day
Your heart bleeding out of control yells for me, and despite the distance, I hear
My bursting veins spew out blood to break the chains
My last few breaths clearly show my pain
But soon, the angel will come and she'll carry us far away together
But, because the angel brings you my heart, forever shall we rest in peace

Last Breath
by Sheila Johnson

How did I get here?
Why am I laying on the cold wet ground?
The only sound I hear is the slowing of my own heart.
I know it's almost time for me to leave.
But right before I do, I see you.
Why I'm thinking about you I have no idea.
You're the one that put me here,
But I can't help it, I still love you.
Although you left me with so many questions,
I will always remember the special times we had.
My last breath I use for you,
To only let you know that I love you.

Awake Again
by Tiffany Koch

The chill of winter dozes off
The leaves of green now shed their frost
They return to brilliance and come to preen
And now embrace a comely sheen
Of showers falling light and balmy
Their beauty to this day enthralls me.
So get up now and out the door,
It's spring in Santa Cruz once more.

Broken Stranger
by Kayla Judd

Strive through pain, through suffering, through trauma and to move on with life
Leave this life behind, where the ocean is tears mixed with blood from my scars
Anger is filled within me, boiling inside, pressure building,
Not sure how long I'll last
Everyday a new part of my heart is shred to pieces by the razor talons of this world
Ceaseless nightmares, pulling, pulling. Drawing thoughts, tormenting my being
Shattering the person I once was and creating a new stranger, a broken stranger
Hiding behind her smile, wishing the best for others, helping others, but not herself
Heartache. One word, so much pain, a physical tremor felt everywhere in my body
Stabbing a thousand times over, knowing it hurts, yet stabbing again and again
Desperately wishing for the pain to end, but with the knowing that it never will
Forced to carry this burden to the end of days, a slave to the hands of torture
Mental images of what was, what could have been, but what will never be
Frantic to make it stop, searching for answers, searching for the end
This is the end of the beginning. Anguish felt to the very ends of my fingertips,
Spreading slowly like poison to the tips of my toes. Killing everything in its path
Unstoppable. Unthinking. Never once looking back in its path of destruction,
As effective as a bullet sent straight to the brain. Broken down, irreparable damage
Damage to me. Lost, wondering,
Confused in this world that rapes the truth and slaughters the good,
Leaving my broken heart in the endless pit of despair.

This Question Lingers
by Loren Martin

This question lingers,
She keeps a secret,
How should you find out,
The question to fate,
The question to date,
How shall the question come,
If she keeps the answer a secret,
A deep dark secret,
Locked away in a box beneath her skin,
She opens it just to wish and find hope,
But you dare not ask,
For you are scared and she is too,
You think she won't show,
But you will soon find ...
You ask the question ...
You ask the one ...
She reaches in and gives you the key
The key to the box and in that box you find no secret ...
But you find her heart, the heart of the one,
The one and only true one, your one true love.

The Reason I Care
by Brandon Henry

I've stopped all my addictions,
I've tried with all my heart,
I've caused many conflictions.
I've drawn for you many works of art.
I've caused us plenty of pain,
Like car wrecks in the pouring rain.
You've given me chances,
You've tried with all your might,
You've gotten plenty of dirty glances.
You've put up a pretty good fight.
You've never done anything wrong,
Maybe I could think of you a love song.
We've made it through disruptions,
We've started to bounce back,
We've stopped causing many interruptions.
We've sealed up most of the cracks.
We've been set on the right track,
Hopefully I won't try to slack.

Can't Bear
by Sara Lloyd

I can't bear to think of you
I can't bear to look at you
And I can't bear to speak to you
But when I even think of forgetting you
My heart breaks
Tears fill my eyes
And I cry for the times that we've shared
The good and the bad
I smile for the laughs that we've shared
Even though it feels as if you never cared
And even though I can't stand to be near you
I find myself wanting to forgive you
But then I remember the bad
The times that you made me so mad and so sad
How I used to drown myself in my tears
And how you mocked all of my fears
So even though I can't bear to look, speak, or even think of you
I can't let myself forget you
Because somewhere along the way, you became a part of me
And I can't forget you or anyone I love

Hope
by Brandi Morris

Hope is a
page in a   book, Hope
is a dream   in the night,
Hope is a   way out of
darkness, Hope   is the red
in a ruby,   Hope is the
black with the   white, Hope is
the war and the fights,
Hope is the freedom of
speech, Hope   is love and
hate, Hope is   a candle with
no flame, Hope   is a picture
in a broken frame,   Hope is the
word of the day,   Hope with
all you   can say

3rd Place

Michael Shupp

Michael is now a senior in high school
and has been named Vice President
of his school's chapter of the National Honor Society.
When he isn't busy studying,
you may find him competing on the varsity soccer or basketball team.
Helping out at church or at home with his two brothers
rounds out this talented author's busy lifestyle.

The Kraken
by Michael Shupp

Far, far beneath the thunderous deep
In the abysmal dark doth sleep
A nameless horror, to be true
Untainted, untouched beneath the blue
Its ancient form most hideous lies
Under rock, and sea and skies
Huge sponges of millennial height
Above it shield from fading light
In depths where never sun has shone,
It waits, unseen and all alone
And many, unknowing, journey past,
Unaware this day shall be their last
They blindly sail o'er quiet water
Heading into gruesome slaughter
Long tentacles grope and fast surround
The ships that suddenly are bound
And down, fast down through roiling waves
The victims pass to nameless graves
Never to reach the distant shore
They lie in darkness evermore

Shelby Lokken

Shelby wrote to us
as a senior in high school.
This 2009 pageant princess
loves animals, writing, and art.
One for giving back to the community,
she runs a non-profit organization
for people with special needs.
Shelby credits the support of her loving family
for all her success.

Lucifer's Clever Joke
by Shelby Lokken

Her eyes snap open to see nothing but the pitch black surrounding her.
Her heart starts to race and her mind is twisting with questions,
But her body will take over, basic human instinct.
Her mouth opens and a blistering scream fights free.
Her newly french manicured nails begin scraping at what they can
Of the silky material above her,
With each nail snapping off and the skin beaten down to the bone.
Her legs are flailing and her toes break in her rich red 5-inch stilettos
With every blow to the container imprisoning her.
Her shrills will be heard by only the lifeless bodies
Peacefully lying around her
And now, her breaths are becoming further apart.
A slow, suffocating death will make Lucifer laugh.
Her life was nothing but a clever joke.

1st Place

Caeli Faisst

Caeli is a busy girl.
She lists her hobbies as reading, writing,
playing the guitar, singing, and sports.
She's also very involved at school
where she takes part in Drama Club
and is a member of Student Council.
It's a wonder that this talented author
still has the time to write such inspirational poetry,
but we're glad she does.
It gives us great pleasure to present "Teenage Eyes" by Caeli Faisst,
this year's Editor's Choice Award Winner.

Editor's Choice Award

Teenage Eyes
by Caeli Faisst

Words jump off the page,
"Outcast," they scream.
Laughing demons circle my head
Taunting me as my tears cause their words to bleed,
Words written from the blackness of their hearts.
They try to fling their words at me,
But I harden my heart and let their flaming arrows bounce off.
Harder and harder they throw their curses,
Harder and harder it is to keep my heart from breaking.
Finally they leave, leave me at peace,
Yet their cruel eyes haunt my vision.
The ink from their words mixed with my tears seeps into my skin,
Mixing its poison with my blood,
But I refuse to accept defeat.
I will rise above.
I will not let them win.

Index of Authors

Index of Authors

Index of Authors

Index of Authors

Index of Authors

The Gold Edition
Price List

Initial Copy 32.95

Additional Copies 24.00

Please Enclose $6 Shipping/Handling Each Order

Check or Money Order Payable to:

The America Library of Poetry
P.O. Box 978
Houlton, Maine 04730

Must specify book title and author

Please Allow 4-6 Weeks For Delivery

THE AMERICA
LIBRARY OF POETRY

www.libraryofpoetry.com

Email: generalinquiries@libraryofpoetry.com

Poetry On the Web

See Your Poetry Online!

This is a special honor reserved exclusively for our published poets.
Now that your work has been forever set in print,
why not share it with the world at www.libraryofpoetry.com

At the America Library of Poetry,
our goal is to showcase quality writing in such a way
as to inspire others to broaden their literary horizons,
and we can think of no better way to reach people around the world
than by featuring poetic offerings like yours on our global website.

Since we already have your poem in its published format,
all you need to do is copy the information from the form below on
a separate sheet of paper, and return it with a $6 posting fee.
This will allow us to display your poetry
on the internet for one full year.

Author's Name _____

Poem Title _____

Book Title _____ *The Gold Edition* _____

Mailing Address _____

City _____ State _____ Zip Code _____

E-mail Address _____

Check or Money Order in the amount of $6 payable to:
The America Library of Poetry
P.O. Box 978
Houlton, Maine 04730